The Ninja Foodi Pressure Cooker Cookbook

100 Fast, Healthy and Wonderful Recipes to Pressure Cook, Slow Cook, Air Fry, Dehydrate, and More

Bernadette Cruz

Copyright 2020 by Bernadette Cruz - All rights reserved.

This document is geared towards providing exact and reliable information in regards to the topic and issue covered. The publication is sold with the idea that the publisher is not required to render accounting, officially permitted, or otherwise, qualified services. If advice is necessary, legal or professional, a practiced individual in the profession should be ordered.

From a Declaration of Principles which was accepted and approved equally by a Committee of the American Bar Association and a Committee of Publishers and Associations.

In no way is it legal to reproduce, duplicate, or transmit any part of this document in either electronic means or in printed format. Recording of this publication is strictly prohibited and any storage of this document is not allowed unless with written permission from the publisher. All rights reserved.

The information provided herein is stated to be truthful and consistent, in that any liability, in terms of inattention or otherwise, by any usage or abuse of any policies, processes, or directions contained within is the solitary and utter responsibility of the recipient reader. Under no circumstances will any legal responsibility or blame be held against the publisher for any reparation, damages, or monetary loss due to the information herein, either directly or indirectly.

Respective authors own all copyrights not held by the publisher.

The information herein is offered for informational purposes solely, and is universal as so. The presentation of the information is without contract or any type of guarantee assurance.

The trademarks that are used are without any consent, and the publication of the trademark is without permission or backing by the trademark owner. All trademarks and brands within this book are for clarifying purposes only and are the owned by the owners themselves, not affiliated with this document.

Table of content

INTRODUCTION 7

CHAPTER ONE BREAKFAST 9

   1. Breakfast omelets 9
   2. Breakfast Burritos 10
   3. Egg Bites 11
   4. Low-Carb Breakfast Casserole 12
   5. Ninja Foodi Donuts 13
   6. Blueberry Lemon Cronuts 14
   7. Buttermilk blueberry breakfast cake 16
   8. Ninja Foodi Bacon 17
   9. Egg and Avocado in the Ninja Food 18
   10. Ninja Foodi Breakfast Pizza 19
   11. Easy Homemade Biscuits 20
   12. Ninja Foodi Apple Cinnamon Oatmeal 21
   13. Breakfast Sandwich Waffle 22
   14. Ninja Foodi Yogurt 23
   15. Copy Cat Egg McMuffin 24
   16. Strawberry Acai Bowl 25
   17. Avocado Toast 26
   18. Huevos Rancheros 27

CHAPTER TWO APPETIZERS & SNACKS 29

   19. Ninja Foodi French Fries 29
   20. Cheesy Cauliflower Gratin 30
   21. Roasted Garlic 31
   22. Blooming Onion 32

23. Reuben Fritters 33

24. Hot Ham and Cheese Pinwheels 34

25. Garlic and Parmesan Zucchini Fries 35

26. Zucchini Fritters 36

27. Chick Fil a Copycat 37

28. Egg Rolls 38

29. Copycat Coconut Shrimp 39

30. Taco Pie 40

31. Ninja Foodi Donuts 41

32. Garlic Butter Steak Bites with Mushroom 42

33. Red Beans and Rice 43

CHAPTER THREE CHICKEN & TURKEY 45

34. Southern Fried Air Fryer Chicken 45

35. Rotisserie Chicken 46

36. Crispy Wings 47

37. Firecracker Chicken 48

38. Chicken Cordon Bleu Meatballs 49

39. Southern Fried Chicken 50

40. Parmesan Crusted Chicken 51

41. Roast Chicken 52

42. Chicken Tenders 53

43. Olive Garden Italian Dressing Chicken 54

44. Whole Turkey in the Ninja Foodi 55

45. Turkey Breast 56

46. Turkey Paprikash 57

47. Orange Blossom Chicken 58

48. Turkey and sweet potatoes 59

49. Healthy Turkey Chili 60

CHAPTER FOUR PORK, BEEF & LAMB 61

50. Pulled Pork BBQ 61
51. Juicy Grilled Pork Chops 62
52. Foodi Buttery Ranch Pork Chops 63
53. Pork Tacos 64
54. Crispy Pork Carnitas 65
55. Pork Chops 66
56. Herb Crusted Pork Chops 67
57. BBQ Pork 68
58. Beef and Cabbage 69
59. Ninja Foodi Picadillo 71
60. BBQ Beef Short Ribs 72
61. Sesame Beef 73
62. Roast Beef 74
64. Beef Taco Soup 76
66. Cheesy Beef and Rice Casserole 78
67. Beef with Rice 79
68. Beef Stew 80
69. Lamb Shanks with Roasted Carrots 81
70. Tomato Fresca Lamb Chops 82
71. Rack of Lamb Kebabs 83
72. Broiling Steak 84
73. Lamb Shanks 85
74. Braised Lamb Shanks with Red Wine 86
75. Lamb with Mint 87
76. Steak and Vegetable Bowls 89
77. Prime Rib in the Ninja Foodi 90
78. Ninja Foodi Steak 91

CHAPTER FIVE FISH & SEAFOOD 93

79. Ninja Foodi Crab Legs 93
80. Ninja Foodi Shrimp Boil 94
81. Cajun Shrimp Boil 95
82. Herbed Salmon Recipe 97
83. Fish and Grits 98
84. Air Fryer Tilapia 99
85. Crumbed Fish 100
86. Beer Battered Fish 101
87. Lobster Tails 102
88. Mahi Mahi with Peach & Arugula Salad 103
89. Fish Recipe Pecan Crusted Halibut 104
90. Air Fryer Catfish 105
91. Crispy Golden Air Fryer Fish 106

CHAPTER SEX DESSERTS 107

92. Chocolate Fondue 107
93. Broiled Bananas 108
94. Grilled Strawberry Shortcake Skewers 109
94. Zeppole 110
95. Coconut Pineapple Sorbet 111
96. Spicy Mango Sorbet 112
97. Mocha 113
98. Lemon Strawberry Sorbet 114
99. Cranberry Salsa over Cream Cheese 115
100. Easy Crème Brulee 116

Introduction

Firstly, thanks and congratulations for choosing to invest in this book!
Are you curious about the Ninja Foodi, a pressure cooker, and air fryer combination device? An air fryer/pressure cooker combo so it piqued many people's curiosity. I have used and cooked with the Ninja Foodi. Using it both as a pressure cooker and as an air fryer and how that works in a single device, I have compiled various tips and tricks of using a ninja foodi. I call it the complete beginner guide to ninja foodi and many more.

Did you just get your new multi function pressure cooker ninja foodi that includes an air fryer? Now you're wondering how to go about these fabulous Ninja cooking system. Well, you just it the right button, as this book is a complete guide for everything you need to use a ninja foodi along with instructions for you plus lots of easy Ninja Foodi recipes too.

The book consist:
Chapter One Breakfast
Chapter Two Appetizers & Snacks
Chapter Three Chicken & turkey
Chapter Four Pork, beef & lamb
Chapter Five Fish & Seafood
Chapter Sex Desserts

No matter what you're in the mood for, the recipes inside this book will cover it all!
These recipes are perfect for beginners, and are quick and easy to prepare... so let's get cooking!

Thanks again for reading this book, I hope you enjoy it!

Chapter One Breakfast

1. Breakfast omelets

TIME TO PREPARE
10 MINUTES

COOK TIME
11 MINUTES

SERVING
4

PREPARED BY
NINJA FOODI

INGREDIENTS

0.5 c onion diced
0.67 tbsp. olive oil
3.33 mushrooms sliced
5.33 eggs scrambled
0.17 cream of mushroom soup could use alfredo sauce too
0.33 tsp garlic salt
0.5 c cheese shredded
0.33 lb. sausage spicy ground sausage is best
0.67 chive diced, optional

STEPS TO COOK

1. Turn your Ninja Foodi on and press sauté. Put in your olive oil, diced onions, and ground sausage (spicy is best) /or bacon.
2. Cook until halfway done, then add sliced mushrooms. Cook until sausage is no longer pink. Press stop on machine. (if there is a lot of grease, drain)
3. In a bowl scramble your eggs and pour into your Ninja Foodi with your meat.
4. Sprinkle in your garlic salt, 1/2 c of shredded cheese, and add 1/4 c cream of mushroom soup or alfredo sauce can be used.
5. Stir together so all of this is combined well.
6. Close your air fryer lid and press air crisp button, 390 degrees for 6 minutes.
7. Lift lid and stir so uncooked egg on bottom is circulated and able to cook thoroughly.
8. Close lid again and set to air crisp, 390 degrees for another 4-5 minutes. Timing now will depend on how well done you like your egg/omelet. Look after 4 minutes and cook until it is the desired consistency.
9. Serve with added cheese on top and a sprinkle of chives.

2. Breakfast Burritos

TIME TO PREPARE
10

COOK TIME
45

SERVING
8

PREPARED BY NINJA FOODI

INGREDIENTS

- 0.67 tsp olive oil
- 0.67 lb. breakfast sausage
- 0.67 medium russet potato about 2 cups
- 1.33 tsp sea salt divided
- 0.67 tsp black pepper divided
- 6.67 large eggs
- 2 cups cheese shredded
- 8 8" flour tortillas

STEPS TO COOK

1. Cut and dice your medium sized Russet potato into 1/2-inch dice. Soak your diced potatoes in cold water for at least 30 minutes.
2. Add 1 tsp of olive oil to the inner pot of the Ninja Foodi and turn the sauté mode to high. Add in 1 lb. of breakfast sausage & sauté the sausage until it is about 1/2 way cooked and the fat begins to render out. This will take about 5-7 minutes.
3. Add the diced and drained potatoes, along with 1 tsp salt and 1/2 tsp of pepper (or whatever spices you want to add) and sauté just until you can pierce the potato, but it is still firm. This takes about 5-7 minutes.
4. While the potatoes and sausage are sautéing, lightly scramble your eggs with 1 tsp salt and 1/2 tsp pepper.
5. Move the potatoes and sausage around so they cover the entire bottom of the inner pot of the Ninja Foodi. Pour in the scrambled eggs and turn off the Sauté mode.
6. Cover the Inner Pot with aluminum foil and punch at least 10 small holes in the top to allow some airflow, but not the full force of the fan. Select the Bake function and set the temperature to 325° F and the time for 20 minutes. After 15 minutes, remove the foil and allow baking the remaining 5 minutes.
7. Remove burrito filling from the inner pot and place into a mixing bowl. Position the rack or basket into the Ninja Foodi and set the Air Crisp to 375° F to pre-heat.
8. Assemble your breakfast burrito. Add 1/2 cup of filling onto one side of the tortilla shell and top with about 1-2 Tbsp. of shredded cheese. See post for tips on rolling the burrito

3. Egg Bites

TIME TO PREPARE
5

COOK TIME
8

SERVING
7

PREPARED BY NINJA FOODI

INGREDIENTS

4 Large eggs
1/4 Cup Cottage cheese
1/2 Cup Shredded cheese
3 Strips of cooked bacon- cut into bite sized pieces
1/4 Cup Heavy whipping cream.
1/4 Teaspoon salt
Non-Stick cooking Spray
1/4 teaspoon Pepper to Taste

STEPS TO COOK

1. Beat eggs, cream, cottage cheese, salt and pepper together until evenly combined. This is super easy in a blender!
2. Lightly spray silicone egg bites mold with non-stick cooking spray.
3. Stuff egg bites mold 1/2 of the way full with egg.
4. Put in a tablespoon of shredded cheese to each egg mold.
5. Put in about 1/2 piece of cooked bacon (in bite-sized pieces) to each egg mold.
6. Mix each egg mold until ingredients are well combined. Cover filled egg bites mold with foil.
7. Pour 1 cup of water into the Ninja Foodi insert pot. Put a trivet into the Ninja Foodi and lower your filled egg bites mold onto the trivet. Or use a silicone sling. You do not need to use a trivet if you use the silicone sling.
8. Close pressure-cooking lid and move valve to "seal" position.
9. Turn Ninja Foodi On and choose pressure cooker setting. Choose "low" and change time to 8 minutes. Push start.
10. If you are cooking more than one tray of egg bites at the same time, add 1 minute for each additional tray.
11. When timer beeps, let pressure naturally release for 5 minutes and then quick release remaining pressure.
12. Open pressure cooker lid and remove egg bites from Ninja Foodi. Remove foil and let cool for 2 minutes. Put a plate on top of egg bites and flip the egg bites onto the plate.
13. Take off the foil and let cool for 2 minutes.
14. Place a plate on top of egg bites and flip the egg bites onto the plate.

4. Low-Carb Breakfast Casserole

TIME TO PREPARE 5	**COOK TIME** 5	**SERVING** 7	**PREPARED BY** NINJA FOODI

INGREDIENTS

- 1 LB Ground Sausage
- 1/4 Cup Diced White Onion
- 1 Diced Green Bell Pepper
- 8 Whole Eggs, Beaten
- 1/2 Cup Shredded Colby Jack Cheese
- 1 Tsp Fennel Seed
- 1/2 Tsp Garlic Salt

STEPS TO COOK

1. If you are using the Ninja Foodi, use the sauté function to brown the sausage in the pot of the Foodi. If you are using an air fryer, you can use a skillet to do this.
2. Add in the onion and pepper and cook along with the ground sausage until the veggies are soft and the sausage is cooked.
3. Using the 8.75-inch pan or the Air Fryer pan, spray it with non-stick cooking spray.
4. Place the ground sausage mixture on the bottom of the pan.
5. Top evenly with cheese.
6. Pour the beaten eggs evenly over the cheese and sausage.
7. Add fennel seed and garlic salt evenly over the eggs.
8. Place the rack in the low position in the Ninja Foodi, and then place the pan on top.
9. Set to Air Crisp for 15 minutes at 390 degrees.
10. If you are using an air fryer, place the dish directly into the basket of the air fryer and cook for 15 minutes at 390 degrees.
11. Carefully remove and serve.

5. Ninja Foodi Donuts

TIME TO PREPARE
5

COOK TIME
4

SERVING
1

PREPARED BY NINJA FOODI

INGREDIENTS

Grands biscuits
2 cups powdered sugar
1/4 cup milk
1 tsp vanilla

STEPS TO COOK

1. Cut a circle in all biscuits (I used the end of a shot glass)
2. Spray with cooking spray
3. Place in your air fryer or Foodi basket in a single layer
4. Cook at 350 on air fry for 4 minutes.
5. In a small bowl mix powdered sugar, milk and vanilla
6. Dip each Donuts in the glaze and set on a wired rack.
7. Serve

6. Blueberry Lemon Cronuts

TIME TO PREPARE
15

COOK TIME
25

SERVING
4

PREPARED BY
NINJA FOODI

INGREDIENTS

8 tablespoons unsalted butter, room temperature
1 cup sugar, set aside 1 tablespoon
1 egg, room temperature
1 tsp. vanilla
2 cups all-purpose flour, 1 3/4 cup set in a small bowl, 1/4 of cup set aside
2 tsp. baking powder
1 tsp. kosher salt
2 cups fresh blueberries
½ cup buttermilk

STEPS TO COOK

1. Using a mixer, cream the butter with 1 cup (less 1 tablespoon) of sugar until light and fluffy.
2. Add the egg and vanilla and mix until combined.
3. Toss the blueberries with ¼ cup of flour to coat the blueberries & set aside.
4. Mix the remaining flour, baking powder and salt.
5. Add half of the flour mixture to the batter, and mix with a spatula, folding to incorporate.
6. Add buttermilk. Stir.
7. Add remaining flour and stir until flour is mixed in. Fold in the blueberries. (Leave excess flour from the blueberry bowl behind.)
8. Spray pot well with canola spray.
9. Pour batter into your pot.

10. Close crisping lid. Select Air Crisp, set temperature to 350 degrees and set time to 25 min. Select Start.
11. Check your cake after about 15 minutes.
12. You will want to keep an eye on your cake to make sure it is not getting to brown on top and is cooking completely through.
13. Your cake should be fully cooked between 20-25 minutes. Check with a toothpick to see when it completely cooked.
14. Enjoy!

7. Buttermilk blueberry breakfast cake

TIME TO PREPARE
16

COOK TIME
30

SERVING
4

PREPARED BY
NINJA FOODI

INGREDIENTS

½ cup unsalted butter
zest from 1 large lemon
214 g sugar
1 egg, room temperature
1 tsp. vanilla
256 g all-purpose flour (set aside 1/4 cup of blueberries)
2 tsp. baking powder
1 tsp. kosher salt (I like 1.25 tsp)
2 cups fresh blueberries, picked over
½ cup buttermilk

STEPS TO COOK

1. Preheat the oven to 350ºF. Using a food processor or hand mixer, cream the butter with the lemon zest and 1 cup minus 1 tablespoon of sugar until light and soft. Put the egg, vanilla, and mix. In the meantime, toss the blueberries with ¼ cup of flour, then beat the remaining flour, baking powder and salt together.
2. Add half of the flour mixture and mix with the spatula to incorporate. Add all of the buttermilk. Stir. Add remaining flour, and stir until flour is absorbed. Fold in the blueberries. (Leave excess flour from the blueberry bowl behind.)
3. Grease an 8- or 9-inch square baking pan (or something similar—I prefer this 8-inch pan because I like the thicker pieces) with butter or coat with non-stick spray. If you have parchment paper on hand, line the pan with parchment on top of the butter. Spread the batter into the pan. Sprinkle the batter with the remaining tablespoon of sugar. Cook for 35 to 45 minutes. (It is not unusual for this cake to take 50 minutes, so just be patient). Let cool at least 15 minutes before serving.

8. Ninja Foodi Bacon

TIME TO PREPARE
3

COOK TIME
12

SERVING
2

PREPARED BY NINJA FOODI

INGREDIENTS	STEPS TO COOK
bacon	1. Place 5-6 slices of bacon in the air crisp basket. 2. Close Air Crisp Lid and press Air Crisp. 3. Set temp to 360 and time to 12 minutes 4. At 12 minutes, check for desired crispness. Cook an additional 1-3 minutes if desired.

9. Egg and Avocado in the Ninja Food

TIME TO PREPARE
5

COOK TIME
12

SERVING
2

PREPARED BY
NINJA FOODI

INGREDIENTS

1 Avocado
Salt and Pepper to taste
Cooking spray and tin foil
2 eggs

STEPS TO COOK

1. Cut avocado in half
2. Scoop some out. (Approx. a teaspoon – a tablespoon)
3. Place a cracked egg in each half of the avocado
4. Add salt and pepper to taste
5. Top with cheese
6. Place on sprayed foil squares and place into air fry basket. AF at 390 for 11-12 minutes Plate and enjoy!
7. Feel free to top with cheese, salsa, hot sauce or any condiment to your liking. You may melt the cheese on top by adding the cheese at the end and an additional minute cook time.

10. Ninja Foodi Breakfast Pizza

TIME TO PREPARE
8

COOK TIME
18

SERVING
6

PREPARED BY NINJA FOODI

INGREDIENTS

For the Biscuit Pizza Dough
1 C (120g) All Purpose Flour
1 Tbsp (12g) Granulated Sugar (I used Swerve)
1 tsp Baking Powder
1/4 tsp Kosher Salt (or 1/8 tsp table salt)
2/3 C (150g) Fat Free Greek Yogurt

For the Toppings
4 slices Center Cut Bacon, cut into thin strips
4 large Eggs, beaten
2 oz. Reduced Fat Cream Cheese, softened or room temp
2 oz. Freshly Shredded Cheese (I used half cheddar, half pepper jack)

STEPS TO COOK

1. Mix the flour, sugar, baking powder, and salt in a large bowl before adding the Greek yogurt. Use a fork to mix until crumbly. Empty the beginnings of the dough onto a flat surface and use your hands to form a ball of dough.
2. Use your knuckles to press outward from the center of the dough, creating thicker edges for the crust than in the center. The dough should be about 8" in diameter. You can also use a rolling pin here.
3. Spray the air fryer basket with cooking spray before adding the crust. Brush the top with a splash of skim milk, egg whites, butter, or a bit more cooking spray.
4. Air fry at 375ºF for 10 minutes before flipping and air frying an additional 3 minutes at 375ºF before adding the toppings.
5. While the crust cooks, add the bacon strips to a nonstick skillet over medium-high heat. Once fully cooked, remove the skillet from the heat and add the eggs. Stir to scramble and add the cream cheese once the eggs are nearly cooked. Set aside. (Optional: set aside some of the cooked bacon pieces before adding the eggs to use as a topping when serving.)
6. Add the bacon and eggs mixture to the crust. Top with the shredded cheese and air fry for an additional 3-5 minutes until the cheese is melted and bubbly. Let the pizza cool for a minute or two before carefully transferring out of the air fryer basket and slicing. Enjoy!

11. Easy Homemade Biscuits

TIME TO PREPARE
11

COOK TIME
11

SERVING
8

PREPARED BY
NINJA FOODI

INGREDIENTS

2 cups flour all purpose, chilled
1/2 tsp sea salt fine grind
1 Tbsp. baking powder
1 Tbsp. granulated white sugar
6 Tbsp. butter salted
1/2 cup Greek yogurt plain, whole fat, unsweetened
1/4 cup water

STEPS TO COOK

1. Select the Bake function on the Ninja Foodi, set the temp for 375° and the time for 20 minutes. Combine flour, salt, baking powder and sugar in a metal mixing bowl or a chilled glass bowl.
2. Remove the butter from the fridge and cut into 1/4 inch slices into the bow with the flour. Use a pastry cutter or fork to combine the flour and butter until it has a very course texture.
3. Make a well in the middle of the flour/butter mixture and pour in the Greek yogurt and water mixture. You should not have a dough yet. See video for details.
4. Dump mixture onto a floured surface and press down with your fingertips until you have a 4"x 4" piece of dough. Fold the top down to the bottom. Rotate 90° and repeat x 5, collecting all the melted flour / butter as you proceed. Each time you press and rotate, make the square bigger, but do not go more than 8" x 8". Don't over work the dough, see post for details.
5. When all the loose flour is incorporated, gently press dough down with your fingers until it is about 1" thick. Press straight down, do not twist.
6. After you get as many biscuits as you can out of that dough, gently bring it back together and press it down again to 1" thick. You should get at least 8 biscuits. I got 10. Only 8 will fit in the Ninja Foodi, but see the post for details on freezing the other two.

12. Ninja Foodi Apple Cinnamon Oatmeal

TIME TO PREPARE
6

COOK TIME
24

SERVING
4

PREPARED BY
NINJA FOODI

INGREDIENTS

1 cup Steel Oats Do not use other oats and they cannot withstand the high temperature.

1 tsp Cinnamon

1 each Apple, cored, peeled and diced Use good cooking apples like Granny Smith.

4 cups Water

STEPS TO COOK

1. Core, peel and dice apple. I use the Pampered Chef Corer as it makes this a breeze.
2. Add oats, apple and cinnamon to the Ninja Foodi.
3. Add water to the Ninja Foodi and stir well.
4. Close pressure top and set to high for 9 minutes.
5. Let pressure naturally release for 15 minutes once complete.
6. Open lid and stir oatmeal. It is very hot, but as you place in bowls add sweetener such as brown sugar, or honey. Add any other toppings desired such as raisins or nuts.

13. Breakfast Sandwich Waffle

TIME TO PREPARE
2

COOK TIME
4

SERVING
2

PREPARED BY
NINJA FOODI

INGREDIENTS

3 Eggs
1/2 Cup Shredded Cheese
1 Tube Crescent Rolls
Cut up Vegetables

STEPS TO COOK

1. Scramble eggs to your liking. Can also be egg whites.
2. Place 3 pieces or crescent roll on your warmed waffle maker. Having some space in between is fine since they are going to puff up a little. You will need to tear off some of each piece to make them fit well. Close lid for 15-30 seconds and just lightly start cooking the crescent rolls.
3. Put shredded cheese on top.
4. Spoon scrambled eggs on top.
5. Put your vegetable on top.
6. Close lid and cook for 1-2 minutes until cook all the way.

14. Ninja Foodi Yogurt

TIME TO PREPARE
6

COOK TIME
8

SERVING
4

PREPARED BY
NINJA FOODI

INGREDIENTS

½ gallon of whole milk
3-4 Tbsp. of plain yogurt

STEPS TO COOK

1. Pour milk into your pot then seal the pot with the lid and seal closed. (If you want to add a 14 oz. can of sweetened condensed milk) you can do so before closing your lid) Push the "keep warm" button and leave milk for about 40-45 minutes.
2. Release the lid and whisk your warm milk.
3. Set the IP to "sauté" to heat the milk to 185 degrees.
4. Once milk hot remove inner pot with hot pads and set aside to cool to 110 degrees.
5. Add 3-4 Tbsp. of plain yogurt in your cooled milk and whisk.

15. Copy Cat Egg McMuffin

TIME TO PREPARE
12

COOK TIME
14

SERVING
2

PREPARED BY
Ninja foodi

INGREDIENTS	STEPS TO COOK
2 Eggs 2 muffins 2 slices bacon 2 slices cheese	1. Preheat air fryer to 400 2. Using 2 rings from the top of a ball mason jar 3. Place foil over the rack 4. spray with cooking oil 5. crack one egg in each jar lid 6. place bacon on the rack 7. cook for 5 minutes and flip the bacon 8. continue cooking for another 5 minutes 9. remove egg 10. Place split muffin in the air fryer and toast for 5 minutes or until brown. 11. Put a slice of cheese on the muffin, egg, and bacon.

16. Strawberry Acai Bowl

TIME TO PREPARE
7

COOK TIME
6

SERVING
2

PREPARED BY
Ninja foodi

INGREDIENTS

2 ½ cups frozen strawberries
2 tablespoons agave nectar
1 1/4 cup vanilla almond milk
2 tablespoons lemon juice
8 fresh mint leaves
1 package (3.5 ounces) frozen acai, thawed

Garnishes
1/4 cup sliced bananas
1/4 cup sliced strawberries
1 teaspoon slivered almonds
1 teaspoon chia seeds
1 tablespoon shredded coconut

STEPS TO COOK

1. Place all ingredients into the 72-ounce pitcher in the order listed.
2. Select ICE CREAM.
3. Add garnishes.

17. Avocado Toast

TIME TO PREPARE
10

COOK TIME
5

SERVING
4

PREPARED BY
Ninja foodi

INGREDIENTS

4 slices bacon, cooked, cooled
2 ripe avocados, pit removed, peeled
1 tablespoon Sriracha sauce
1 tablespoon fresh lime juice
1/4 teaspoon kosher salt
1/4 teaspoon ground pepper
4 slices whole wheat bread, toasted

STEPS TO COOK

1. Place the Total Crushing & Power Chopping Blade into the Jar, then add cooked bacon.
2. Beat 3 times, then transfer chopped bacon to a small bowl.
3. Add avocado, Sriracha, lime juice, salt, and pepper to the jar. Pulse 7 times, then run continuously for 20 seconds.
4. Top each slice of toasted bread with approximately 2 tablespoons avocado spread and chopped bacon.

18. Huevos Rancheros

TIME TO PREPARE 12 **COOK TIME** 12 **SERVING** 4 **PREPARED BY NINJA FOODI**

INGREDIENTS

- 1 tablespoon plus 2 teaspoons canola oil, divided
- 1 small onion, peeled, diced
- 3 cloves garlic, peeled, roughly chopped
- 1 can (15.5 ounces) black beans, rinsed, drained
- 3 teaspoons kosher salt, divided
- 1/2 teaspoon ground cumin
- 1/4 cup water
- 6 large eggs, beaten
- 1/2 cup queso fresco, crumbled, divided
- 4 corn tostadas (6 inches each)
- 1 cup fresh or chunky salsa
- 1/4 cup fresh cilantro, finely chopped
- 1 avocado, peeled, pit removed, thinly sliced

STEPS TO COOK

1. Select SEAR/SAUTÉ and set to MD: HI. Select START/STOP to begin. Allow to preheat for 5 minutes.
2. Add 1 tablespoon oil and onion to pot and sauté for 3 minutes. Add garlic and sauté for 1 minute.
3. Add beans, 1 teaspoon salt, cumin, and water to pot and stir to incorporate.
4. Select PRESSURE and set to HIGH. Set time to 3 minutes. Select START/STOP to begin.
5. While beans are cooking, combine 1/4 cup queso fresco and remaining salt with the beaten eggs.
6. When pressure cooking is complete, quick release the pressure by moving the pressure release valve to the VENT position.
7. Remove beans from the pot and transfer to a small mixing bowl, mashing lightly with a fork.
8. Select SEAR/SAUTÉ and set to MD: HI. Select START/STOP to begin. Put remaining oil, then pour in the egg mixture.
9. Cook eggs, stirring constantly, for about 3 minutes, or until scrambled. Remove eggs from pot.
10. To serve, spread mashed bean mixture onto each tostada, then add eggs, salsa, and avocado. Garnish with remaining queso fresco and cilantro.

Chapter Two Appetizers & Snacks

19. Ninja Foodi French Fries

TIME TO PREPARE
15

COOK TIME
23

SERVING
6

PREPARED BY
Ninja foodi

INGREDIENTS

5 medium potatoes russet, 1.5 lbs.
3 tbsp. olive oil
1/2 tsp seasoned salt

STEPS TO COOK

1. Wash, dry, and slice potatoes into strips (like French fries), leave skins on.
2. Put them in a bowl and rub olive oil on them.
3. Place them into the air fryer basket in your Ninja Foodi or other air fryer machine. (can add some seasoning at this time, we prefer to season at the end)
4. Close lid (one that is attached), turn machine on.
5. Press the air crisp button. Set temp. to 390 for 20-23 minutes. Flip 3 times during total cook time (so every 7 minutes or so).
6. Add a few minutes extra if you want them browner/crispier or take out earlier if you want them very lightly browned. Remove immediately when done for best results.
7. Salt and serve.

20. Cheesy Cauliflower Gratin

TIME TO PREPARE
30

COOK TIME
10

SERVING
4

PREPARED BY
Ninja foodi

INGREDIENTS

250ml beer
2 teaspoons sea salt
40g dried currants or raisins
65g grated Parmesan cheese

STEPS TO COOK

1. Pour beer into the pot. Add the cauliflower, salt, nutmeg and currants. Mount the pressure cover, making sure that the pressure release valve is in the SEAL position.
2. Select PRESSURE and set to HIGH. Set time to 2 minutes. Select START/STOP to begin.
3. While cauliflower mixture is cooking, stir together breadcrumbs and cheese; set aside. In a separate bowl, stir together the cream and flour.
4. When pressure-cooking is complete, quick release the pressure by moving the pressure release valve to the VENT position. Carefully remove the cover when the unit has finished relieving pressure.
5. Add flour mixture to the pot. Select SEAR/SAUTÉ and set to Medium. Select START/STOP to begin. Bring sauce to a boil. Once boiling, press the Power button to turn off SEAR/SAUTÉ.
6. Sprinkle breadcrumb mixture over the cauliflower. Spray with cooking spray.
7. Close crisping lid. Select AIR CRISP, set temperature to 200°C, and set time to 10 minutes. Select START/STOP to begin. Cook until top is golden brown.

21. Roasted Garlic

TIME TO PREPARE	COOK TIME	SERVING	PREPARED BY
5	35	4	NINJA FOODI

INGREDIENTS

Five bulbs garlic you can use less or more and that will not change anything else about the recipe.

1 Tbsp. olive oil I never measure, but this is a good estimate

STEPS TO COOK

1. Cut the stem end of the garlic about ½" down to expose the garlic cloves. Place the bulbs on a sheet of foil or parchment. Drizzle with olive oil to coat the tops. Close the pouch and place in the basket.
2. Close the Tender Crisp lid, select the bake function on 325°F/163°C, and bake for 35 minutes. Open the pouch to make sure garlic is soft and brown. If you want a little more browning, leave the pouch, open and bake at 325°F/163°C in 5-minute increments until it is done.
3. Allow to cool and then either store the bulb in an airtight container in the fridge or squeeze the cloves out and store or freeze.
4. Add the roasted garlic to your favorite dishes and enjoy!

22. Blooming Onion

TIME TO PREPARE
2 HOURS

COOK TIME
20

SERVING
2

PREPARED BY
Ninja foodi

INGREDIENTS

large onion
2 eggs
2 tbsp milk
1 cup panko bread crumbs
1 tsp paprika
1 tsp garlic powder
Olive oil

STEPS TO COOK

1. Peel onion, cut off top. Place cut side down
2. Starting 1/2 inch from the root, cut downward. Cut 8 slices all the way around.
3. Place onion Face down in ice cold water for 2 hours
4. Beat together egg and milk
5. In a separate bowl mix bread crumbs and seasonings
6. Coat onion with egg mixture make sure you get all petals. Tip over to allow all access to drip off.
7. Sprinkle panko all over the onion getting all of the onion.
8. Place in the basket of your Ninja Foodi or air Fryer.
9. Spray with olive oil or cooking spray
10. Cook on air crisp 390 degrees for 10 minutes.
11. Check if it's done if not crispy enough for your liking add an additional 5 minutes

23. Reuben Fritters

TIME TO PREPARE
25

COOK TIME
16

SERVING
2

PREPARED BY
NINJA FOODI

INGREDIENTS

1/2-pound corned beef
1/2 Pound Swiss cheese
4 oz. Cream Cheese
1/2 cup panko bread crumbs
1/2 cup regular bread crumbs
2 eggs
1 cup flour
1/2 tsp garlic powder
Olive Oil spray

STEPS TO COOK

1. Mix together cream cheese, leftover corned beef, and Swiss cheese.
2. Roll into 1" balls
3. Place in freezer for 20 minutes
4. while waiting for balls mix together flour and garlic powder
5. whisk eggs
6. mix together bread crumbs
7. Now Dip each ball in flour, egg, then bread crumbs
8. continue until each ball is well coated
9. Preheat air fryer to 390
10. Place in a single layer and spray with olive oil
11. Cook for 10 minutes and flip over, cook for an additional 5 minutes.

24. Hot Ham and Cheese Pinwheels

TIME TO PREPARE
6

COOK TIME
16

SERVING
2

PREPARED BY
Ninja foodi

INGREDIENTS

Puff pastry
1/2-pound hot ham deli sliced
1/2-pound Monterey jack cheese
Spicy mustard

STEPS TO COOK

1. Preheat air fryer to 400
2. Lay your pastry puff flat
3. Spread a thin layer of mustard
4. Spread a layer of ham
5. a layer of cheese on top of the ham
6. Roll the pastry roll up
7. Slice in 1" slices
8. in a single layer place in your air fryer
9. Cook for 15 minutes in your air fryer flipping over one time after 10 minutes.

25. Garlic and Parmesan Zucchini Fries

TIME TO PREPARE
10

COOK TIME
15

SERVING
4

PREPARED BY
Ninja foodi

INGREDIENTS

1 Large Zucchini
2 eggs
1 Cup flour
1 tbsp garlic powder
1 Cup panko bread crumbs
1/4 cup Parm cheese
Cooking Olive Oil Spray

STEPS TO COOK

1. Cut Zucchini lengthwise in half
2. Cut those both in half as well
3. Cut into fries' strips about 1" long and 1" thick
4. Set Aside
5. whisk 2 eggs in a small bowl
6. place one cup of flour with garlic powder on a small plate or bowl
7. Place panko bread crumbs in another dish with Parm cheese
8. Working in batches first dip each zucchini fry into flour
9. Next into egg
10. last in panko bread crumbs
11. Place your Air Fryer on 375
12. Spray with cooking oil I used olive oil
13. Cook for 15 minutes flipping once after 10 minutes.

26. Zucchini Fritters

TIME TO PREPARE
6

COOK TIME
15

SERVING
4

PREPARED BY
NINJA FOODI

INGREDIENTS

2 Zucchini's
1 cup shredded cheddar
1 egg
1/2 cup flour
2 tbsp chives
1 tsp salt
1 tsp pepper

STEPS TO COOK

1. Shred Zucchinis and squeeze out excess water with a cheesecloth
2. Add zucchini, egg, flour, chives, salt, and pepper to a bowl.
3. Mix together.
4. Make 8 patties with the mixture
5. Optional (place in the freezer for 5-10 minutes) to keep the form
6. Place air fryer on 350
7. Put zucchini patties in the air fryer for 5 minutes
8. Flip over the Pattie for an additional 5-10 minutes or until brown.

27. Chick Fil a Copycat

TIME TO PREPARE
6

COOK TIME
25

SERVING
1

PREPARED BY
Ninja foodi

INGREDIENTS

1-pound chicken breast
1 cup Pickle juice
1 cup flour
1 tsp garlic powder
1 tsp paprika
1 tsp basil
1 tsp salt
1 tsp pepper
1 tbsp peanut oil
1/2 cup milk
1 egg

STEPS TO COOK

1. Cut Chicken breast into 4 pieces.
2. Marinate chicken breast in pickle juice for one hour.
3. Mix together dry ingredients
4. Whisk egg and milk together
5. Dip chicken in flour mixture then egg.
6. Dip back in flour until well coated with flour.
7. Place Air Fryer on 390 preheat for 5 minutes
8. Place chicken pieces on rack in the foodi or air fryer
9. Spray with peanut oil
10. Cook for 20 minutes
11. check temp of your chicken should be 160 degrees

28. Egg Rolls

TIME TO PREPARE
6

COOK TIME
10

SERVING
4

PREPARED BY
Ninja foodi

INGREDIENTS

Egg roll in a bowl
Egg Roll Wrappers
1 Egg
1 tbsp water
Olive oil

STEPS TO COOK

1. Preheat Air Fryer to 390 for 5 minutes
2. Whisk egg and water together
3. Place Egg Roll Mixture in your wrapper.
4. Seal edges with egg mixture
5. Spray egg rolls with olive oil
6. Place in your air fryer basket for 10 minutes or until golden brown

29. Copycat Coconut Shrimp

TIME TO PREPARE
10

COOK TIME
10

SERVING
2

PREPARED BY
Ninja foodi

INGREDIENTS

1 Pound large shrimp
1 cup panko bread crumbs
1 cup shredded coconut
1 cup flour
2 eggs
Olive oil cooking spray

STEPS TO COOK

1. Preheat air fryer to 400 degrees
2. Mix together panko and coconut
3. Whisk 2 eggs
4. First Dip each shrimp in flour
5. Next dip in egg
6. Last dip in panko coconut mix
7. continue doing this until all shrimp are coated
8. Place in a single layer in your air fryer
9. Spray lightly with cooking oil spray
10. Cook for 5 minutes then flip over shrimp
11. Cook for 5 more minutes or until golden brown on each side

30. Taco Pie

TIME TO PREPARE
10

COOK TIME
5

SERVING
2

PREPARED BY
NINJA FOODI

INGREDIENTS

6 Tortilla Shells
1 can refried beans
1-pound ground beef
2 cups cheddar cheese
Taco Seasonings

STEPS TO COOK

1. Spray bottom of fat daddio or spring form pan with cooking spray
2. Cook ground beef over a medium heat until brown and crumbled
3. Add taco seasonings and water per directions.
4. Add a tortilla shell to the bottom of the pan.
5. Spread a thin layer of refried beans.
6. Top with a layer of taco meat
7. Next layer with cheese
8. Repeat steps till your pan is full.
9. Finally, top with a tortilla shell and top with lots of cheese
10. Place in the bottom of your air fryer or Ninja Foodi
11. Cook on air crisp at 400 for 5 minutes.

31. Ninja Foodi Donuts

TIME TO PREPARE
5

COOK TIME
4

SERVING
2

PREPARED BY NINJA FOODI

INGREDIENTS

Grands biscuits
2 cups powdered sugar
1/4 cup milk
1 tsp vanilla

STEPS TO COOK

1. Cut a circle in all biscuits (I used the end of a shot glass)
2. Spray with cooking spray
3. Place in your air fryer or foodi basket in a single layer
4. Cook at 350 on air fry for 4 minutes.
5. In a small bowl mix powdered sugar, milk and vanilla
6. Dip each donut in the glaze and set on a wired rack.
7. Serve

32. Garlic Butter Steak Bites with Mushroom

TIME TO PREPARE   **COOK TIME**   **SERVING**   **PREPARED BY**
6   10   2   NINJA FOODI

INGREDIENTS

1 Tbsp Olive Oil
2 pounds New York Strip Steak
16 oz. white mushrooms
1 tbsp salt
1 tbsp pepper
1 cup Garlic Butter

Garlic Butter
2 Sticks Butter
1 tbsp olive oil
6 cloves chopped garlic
2 tbsp fresh parsley chopped
1 tbsp Fresh thyme
1 tbsp Fresh Rosemary

STEPS TO COOK

1. Place Instant Pot on High Sauté.
2. Add olive oil
3. Cut up steak into 1" cubes (I used NY Strip) you can use any steak you like
4. Add Steak
5. Add Salt and Pepper
6. Cook on sauté until brown
7. Add Garlic Butter and Mushrooms
8. Place your air fryer top on the instant pot
9. Cook on-air crisp at 400 degrees for 10 minutes

For Garlic Butter:
1. In a small bowl mix butter and olive oil until smooth.
2. Add garlic, rosemary, parsley, and thyme.
3. Mix until the butter is smooth.

33. Red Beans and Rice

TIME TO PREPARE 6	**COOK TIME** 1H30	**SERVING** 4	**PREPARED BY NINJA FOODI**

INGREDIENTS

- 2 tbsp olive oil
- 2 cloves garlic
- 1 Onion Chopped
- Dry Red Beans 16 oz.
- 2 tbsp Liquid Smoke
- 2 tbsp Slap Yo Mama Seasoning or Cajun seasoning
- 1 tbsp cayenne pepper
- 1 tbsp chili powder
- 1 tbsp red pepper flakes
- 2 Cups Cooked Rice
- 6 Cups Chicken or ham broth

STEPS TO COOK

1. Place Pot on Sauté
2. Add Olive Oil, garlic, and onions
3. Add dry beans,
4. Add broth, Liquid Smoke, and Seasonings
5. Stir
6. Place on Manual High Pressure for 90 Minutes
7. Do a natural release for 20 minutes
8. Serve over rice

Chapter Three Chicken & turkey

34. Southern Fried Air Fryer Chicken

TIME TO PREPARE
10

SERVING
2

COOK TIME
40

PREPARED BY
Ninja foodi

INGREDIENTS

Whole Cut up chicken
2 cups buttermilk
2 cups all-purpose flour
2 tbsp garlic powder
1 tabs cayenne pepper
2 tabs paprika
1 tabs salt
1 tabs pepper

STEPS TO COOK

1. Take your cut up chicken and place it in buttermilk.
2. marinate the chicken in the buttermilk for 12-24 hours
3. Preheat your air fryer to 350 degrees
4. Stir together your flour and seasoning.
5. Remove chicken from the buttermilk letting excess milk drip off
6. Coat each piece of chicken in the flour mixture
7. Place in a single layer in your air fryer
8. spray chicken with a light coat of olive oil.
9. Cook for 20 minutes
10. flip chicken and cook for an additional 20 minutes
11. Check the temp of your chicken to make sure it's 165 degrees.

35. Rotisserie Chicken

TIME TO PREPARE
5

COOK TIME
45

SERVING
4

PREPARED BY
Ninja foodi

INGREDIENTS

6-pound chicken
3 tbsp olive oil
3 tbsp McCormick Rotisserie seasonings
1 small Onion
2 cloves garlic
1 cup Chicken Broth

STEPS TO COOK

1. Rinse and pat dry your whole chicken
2. Rub olive oil on the skin
3. Rub Rotisserie seasoning all over the chicken both sides.
4. 1 cup broth, garlic and onion directly in your pot
5. Place the chicken in the fryer basket in your Ninja Foodi or if you have the instant pot place directly in your pot
6. Place on high pressure for 30 minutes
7. Do a Quick release
8. Place your air crisp lid on
9. Set to air crisp 400 degrees for 15 minutes or until skin is golden brown.
10. If you have an instant pot remove from pot and place in the broiler to brown the skin.
11. Make sure Chicken is 160 degrees

36. Crispy Wings

TIME TO PREPARE 6	**COOK TIME** 30	**SERVING** 4	**PREPARED BY NINJA FOODI**

INGREDIENTS

2.5 pounds Frozen Chicken Wings
1 cup water
1 cup Franks red hot sauce
1 Stick Butter

STEPS TO COOK

1. Place one cup water in the bottom of your pot.
2. Place wings in your fry basket insert if you have a foodi.
3. Place on a trivet if you have an instant pot
4. Cook on high pressure for 10 minutes
5. Do a quick release
6. Remove your pressure lid and use the air crisp lid on 400 for 20 minutes
7. Open every 5 minutes to check for crispness of your desire.
8. In a separate bowl Melt butter and mix with hot sauce
9. place wings in bowl with sauce and coat well Serve

37. Firecracker Chicken

 TIME TO PREPARE
6

 COOK TIME
10

 SERVING
2

 PREPARED BY NINJA FOODI

INGREDIENTS

- 2 tsp sesame oil
- 2 Pounds Chicken cut in 1"cubes
- 1 cup flour
- 1 cup Franks Hot Sauce
- 2 tsp apple cider vinegar
- 1 tsp red pepper flakes
- 3/4 cup Brown Sugar

STEPS TO COOK

1. Cut chicken into 1" pieces
2. Coat chicken in flour
3. Place Instant Pot on Sauté
4. Add sesame oil
5. Add a single layer of chicken
6. Cook chicken until all sides are white
7. You may have to do in batches I had to do 2 batches.
8. Remove Chicken
9. Add Hot Sauce, Apple cider vinegar
10. Add red pepper flakes and brown sugar.
11. Add chicken back in pot
12. Cook on manual high pressure for 10 minutes.
13. Do a quick release.
14. Serve over rice.

38. Chicken Cordon Bleu Meatballs

TIME TO PREPARE
15

COOK TIME
20

SERVING
4

PREPARED BY
NINJA FOODI

INGREDIENTS

1-pound ground chicken or turkey
6 slices deli ham
6 slices Swiss cheese
1 egg
1 cup bread crumbs
1 tbsp ground mustard
1 cup panko bread crumbs

STEPS TO COOK

1. Mix together ground chicken, egg, breadcrumbs, and ground mustard.
2. Shape into 1" balls
3. Press the center of each meatball
4. Add ham and Swiss cheese into the center and reshape into balls.
5. Roll each ball in panko bread crumbs
6. Place ninja foodi on 350
7. Cook for 20 minutes turning over once halfway through
8. Serve with your favorite cheese sauce or dipping sauce.

39. Southern Fried Chicken

TIME TO PREPARE
15

COOK TIME
40

SERVING
4

PREPARED BY
NINJA FOODI

INGREDIENTS

Whole Cut up chicken
2 cups buttermilk
2 cups all-purpose flour
2 tbsp garlic powder
1 tbsp cayenne pepper
2 tbsp paprika
1 tbsp salt
1 tbsp pepper

STEPS TO COOK

1. Take your cut up chicken and place it in buttermilk.
2. marinate the chicken in the buttermilk for 12-24 hours
3. Preheat your air fryer to 350 degrees
4. Stir together your flour and seasoning.
5. Remove chicken from the buttermilk letting excess milk drip off
6. Coat each piece of chicken in the flour mixture
7. Place in a single layer in your air fryer
8. spray chicken with a light coat of olive oil.
9. Cook for 20 minutes
10. flip chicken and cook for an additional 20 minutes
11. Check the temp of your chicken to make sure it's 165 degrees.

40. Parmesan Crusted Chicken

TIME TO PREPARE
5

COOK TIME
15

SERVING
4

PREPARED BY
Ninja foodi

INGREDIENTS

2 Large Chicken breasts
1 cup Parmesan shredded
1 cup panko bread crumbs
1 cup real mayonnaise

STEPS TO COOK

1. Split chicken breasts in half
2. Pound each piece with a meat hammer (so they are even)
3. Spread Mayo on both sides of each piece of chicken
4. Mix together Panko and Parmesan (for keto skip the panko)
5. Coat each piece of chicken in the panko/parmesan mixture
6. Preheat ninja Foodi to 390
7. In a single layer place in air fryer
8. Cook for 15 minutes turning once after 10 minutes.

41. Roast Chicken

TIME TO PREPARE **COOK TIME** **SERVING** **PREPARED BY NINJA FOODI**

INGREDIENTS

- 1 whole chicken, (3.5 - 4 lbs.)
- 1 cup water
- 2 drops liquid smoke
- as desired salt and pepper
- 2 tbsp butter
- 1 tsp paprika, (can used smoked paprika if you wish)
- 1 tsp garlic powder
- 1/2 tsp onion powder
- 1 tsp seasoned salt, (your favorite brand)
- as desired, pepper
- 1/4 cup flour
- 2 cup chicken stock
- 2 tbsp butter
- dash of garlic powder
- as desired, seasoning salt and pepper

STEPS TO COOK

1. Wash and pat dry the chicken. Season inside and out with seasoned salt, pepper, paprika, garlic and onion powders. Set inside the Air Frying basket.
2. Mix the water and the liquid smoke together and pour into the main pot of the Foodi
3. Place the chicken in the basket, inside the main pot of the Foodi
4. Cook on high pressure for 15 minutes.
5. When time is done, do a quick release, remove the chicken and the basket, and discard the water that was in the bottom of the Foodi bowl.
6. Replace the chicken and the basket inside the Foodi liner and place the liner back into the unit.
7. In a small bowl, melt the butter and make up the basting butter recipe above.
8. Air crisp at 400 degrees for 15 minutes. Lifting the lid occasionally, basting the chicken with your basting butter to crisp/brown it to your desired color.
9. Remove the chicken and the basket and cover with a tin foil to continue cooking to reach a temperature reading of 165 degrees.
10. In the Foodi bowl, add the butter and flour to the drippings and press "sauté". Mix everything together and slowly add the stock in small increments as it thickens. When all the liquid is added and thickened, you are ready to serve!
11. Enjoy!

42. Chicken Tenders

TIME TO PREPARE
10

COOK TIME
15

SERVING
4

PREPARED BY
Ninja foodi

INGREDIENTS	STEPS TO COOK
1.33 lbs. chicken tenders 0.33 c ketchup 0.33 c brown sugar 0.67 tsp onion powder 0.67 tsp paprika 0.67 tsp salt 0.33 tsp pepper olive oil spray	1. Combine ketchup, brown sugar, onion powder, paprika, salt, and pepper in a medium mixing bowl. 2. Set aside 1/4 cup of sauce for later. Put chicken tenders to the sauce making sure they are completely covered. 3. Allow to soak in marinade/sauce for 15 minutes. Put chicken tenders in a greased air fryer basket. Preheat air fryer for 5 minutes once they're marinated. 4. Spray inside of basket with olive oil spray. Ninja foodi at 400 degrees for 10 minutes. Flip tenders over and air fry for an additional 4-6 minutes or until internal temperature reaches 160 degrees in the middle. 5. Brush with remaining BBQ sauce prior to serving.

43. Olive Garden Italian Dressing Chicken

TIME TO PREPARE
8

COOK TIME
12

SERVING
4

PREPARED BY
NINJA FOODI

INGREDIENTS

- 2-3 Large boneless skinless chicken breasts
- 2 Cups Olive Garden Italian salad dressing
- 1/3 Cup grated parmesan cheese

STEPS TO COOK

1. Pour one cup of Olive Garden Italian Dressing into the Ninja Foodi pot.
2. Place 2-3 large boneless skinless chicken breasts into the Ninja Foodi pot.
3. 1 cup of Olive Garden Italian Dressing with 1/3 cup of grated parmesan cheese.
4. Pour dressing/cheese mixture over chicken breasts.
5. Close "pressure cooking" lid and move valve to "seal position."
6. Turn Ninja Foodi "on."
7. Select "pressure cooker" setting and cook on high for 10 minutes.
8. When timer beeps, allow pressure to natural release for 5 minutes.
9. Quick release remaining pressure.
10. Serve with your favorite pasta and vegetables!

44. Whole Turkey in the Ninja Foodi

TIME TO PREPARE	COOK TIME	SERVING	PREPARED BY
10	15	8	NINJA FOODI

INGREDIENTS

Seasoning Blend for Turkey Rub
- 4 Tbsp paprika
- 4 tsp sea salt
- 2 tsp poultry seasoning
- 2 tsp red pepper flakes
- 2 tsp garlic powder
- 2 tsp black pepper course
- 1 tsp rosemary dried

For the Turkey
- 8 lb. turkey
- 2 stalks celery
- 4 cloves garlic
- ½ onion
- 1 orange
- 3 sprigs rosemary

STEPS TO COOK

1. Pat the turkey dry after rinsing. Stuff the cavity with the celery, onion, peeled garlic cloves, orange slices, and rosemary.
2. Rub the seasoning blend all over the turkey. You won't use all of it, but reserve the rest for later.
3. Put the turkey on a silicone sling or you make one out of foil.
4. Add ½ cup of water into the inner pot. Lower the sling with the turkey into the inner pot.
5. Put the pressure lid on and turn the valve to seal. Select high pressure and set the time to 15 minutes. See notes additional information on timing.
6. Leave the turkey natural for 15 minutes, then release the residual pressure.
7. Check the temperature, it should read at least 160° F. If the temperature has not reached 160° F, you can bring it up to the correct temperature by roasting. The temperature will rise an additional 5-10° during the crisping or while it rests if you are skipping that step.
8. Carve and serve the turkey! See post for carving instructions. Enjoy!

45. Turkey Breast

TIME TO PREPARE 10   **COOK TIME** 1H   **SERVING** 4   **PREPARED BY NINJA FOODI**

INGREDIENTS

3 Pound Boneless Turkey Breast
1/2 Tbsp Rosemary
Olive Oil Spray

STEPS TO COOK

1. Place the turkey breast in the basket of the Ninja Foodi or Air Fryer.
2. Coat it with olive oil spray and rosemary.
3. Cook at 350 degrees for 20 minutes.
4. Carefully turn the turkey breast, coat it again with olive oil spray and a dash of rosemary if you prefer.
5. Cook for an additional 30 minutes at 350 degrees.
6. Be sure the internal temperature reaches at least 165 degrees.
7. Let it sit in the Ninja Foodi or Air Fryer for 10-15 minutes after cooking to rest.
8. Slice and serve.

46. Turkey Paprikash

TIME TO PREPARE
5

COOK TIME
40

SERVING
4

PREPARED BY
NINJA FOODI

INGREDIENTS

- 2 bone-in turkey legs (about 2 pounds)
- 2 bone-in turkey thighs (about 3 pounds)
- 4 cloves garlic, peeled
- 2 tablespoons sweet smoked Hungarian paprika
- 1/4 cup brine liquid from pickled jalapeños
- 1 tablespoon kosher salt
- 1 cup beer
- 1 cup sour cream
- 2 tablespoons instant flour

STEPS TO COOK

1. Place all ingredients, except sour cream and flour, into the pot. Mount the pressure cover, making sure that the pressure release valve is in the SEAL position.
2. Select PRESSURE and set to HIGH. Set time to 20 minutes. Select START/STOP to begin.
3. When pressure cooking is complete, quick release the pressure by moving the pressure release valve to the VENT position.
4. Rotate the turkey parts so they are skin-side up.
5. Close the crisping lid. Select BROIL and set time to 15 minutes. Press START/STOP to begin. Cook until skin is blistered, brown, and crisp.
6. When cooking is complete, remove turkey from the sauce and set aside to rest. From here you can either shred the turkey once cool and reheat in the sauce or drizzle the sauce over the turkey.
7. Select SEAR/SAUTÉ and set to HIGH. Select START/STOP to begin. Add sour cream and flour to the liquid in the pot, whisking constantly. Bring mixture to a boil. Once boiling, press the START/STOP button to cancel SEAR/SAUTÉ. Ladle the sauce over the turkey and serve.

47. Orange Blossom Chicken

TIME TO PREPARE
15

COOK TIME
45

SERVING
4

PREPARED BY
Ninja foodi

INGREDIENTS

2 oranges
1 whole chicken (about 3 pounds)
2 tablespoons kosher salt
1 tablespoon sugar
1 cup cream
1 cup chicken broth
1 tablespoon instant flour

STEPS TO COOK

1. Cut the oranges in half. Zest and juice both oranges in a small mixing bowl, reserving the juiced halves. Stuff the orange halves in to the cavity of the chicken.
2. Add the salt, sugar, and cream to a bowl; mix until combined.
3. Place the chicken in a zip-top bag along with the cream mixture and orange zest and juice. Marinade the chicken overnight or up to 24 hours.
4. Pour the chicken broth into the pot.
5. Place the Cook & Crisp™ Basket in the pot. Remove chicken from marinade and place in basket. Mount the pressure cover, making sure that the pressure release valve is in the SEAL position.
6. Select PRESSURE and set to HIGH. Set time to 15 minutes. Select START/STOP to begin.
7. When pressure cooking is complete, quick release the pressure by moving the pressure release valve to the VENT position.
8. Close the crisping lid. Select AIR CRISP, set temperature to 390°F, and set time to 20 minutes. Press START/STOP to begin.
9. When cooking is complete, remove chicken and set aside to rest.
10. Select SEAR/SAUTÉ and set to HIGH. Select START/STOP to begin. Add instant flour to the liquid in the pot, whisking constantly. Bring mixture to a boil. Once boiling, press the Power button to turn off SEAR/SAUTÉ. Ladle the sauce over the chicken and serve.

48. Turkey and sweet potatoes

TIME TO PREPARE
15

COOK TIME
45

SERVING
5

PREPARED BY NINJA FOODI

INGREDIENTS

12 oz. Turkey Breast
1 tbsp garlic powder
1 tbsp smoked paprika
1/2 tsp salt
1/2 tsp oregano
1 tbsp butter
3/4 cup chicken stock

SWEET POTATOES
3 medium sweet potatoes
2 tbsp heavy whipping cream
1 tsp cinnamon
1/4 cup non-fat milk

STEPS TO COOK

TURKEY
1. Open turkey breast and place in a bowl
2. Rub turkey breast with half of the seasonings ensure you get seasonings under the skin of the turkey breast.
3. Pour chicken stock into the Ninja Foodie
4. Place the reversible rack in the down (lower) position
5. Put the turkey breast on its side in the center of the rack
6. Place the sweet potatoes around the turkey breast
7. Put the Ninja Foodie on high for 13 minutes' press start
8. While turkey is cooking mix the other half of the seasonings with melted butter
9. Natural release for 8 minutes then quick release
10. Remove sweet potatoes
11. Remove turkey pour out the juices and set aside if you would like to make gravy with it we didn't.
12. Baste turkey with butter mixture (use a brush to coat the turkey evenly)
13. Close crisping lid adjust temp to 390 degrees for 16 minutes
14. After 8 minutes' flip turkey breast over baste the other side with the remaining butter mixture. close lid and crisp for the remaining 8 minutes (We had some butter mixture left over but we still counted the points. You can add it to your sweet potatoes if you would like)

SWEET POTATOES
1. Mash the sweet potatoes add cinnamon, heavy cream and nonfat milk* mix well
2. Add nonfat milk until you get the consistency you prefer. I used a little less than 1/4 cup.
3. Serve this delicious meal and enjoy the compliments

49. Healthy Turkey Chili

TIME TO PREPARE
5

COOK TIME
25

SERVING
4

PREPARED BY
NINJA FOODI

INGREDIENTS

1 celery stalks diced
0.5 onion diced
0.5 green pepper diced
0.5 lb. lean ground turkey
0.5 cup kale chopped
1 cloves garlic minced
1 14oz cans fire-roasted tomatoes
0.5 14oz can black beans drained and rinsed
1 tbsps. tomato paste
0.5 tbsp chili powder
1 tsps. cumin
0.5 tsp oregano
0.5 tsp sea salt
0.25 tsp pepper
0.13 tsp cayenne
0.13 tsp cinnamon
0.5 cup chicken broth
toppings: avocado, Greek yogurt, cheddar

STEPS TO COOK

1. Please read the notes below to see if you should cook the ground turkey first.
2. Put all of the ingredients to the pot. Put on the lid, seal and cook on high pressure for 25 minutes. Let it manually release (takes roughly 25 minutes). Serve with optional avocado, Greek yogurt, or cheddar cheese.
3. Stove Top Instructions
4. Heat a medium stockpot over medium-high heat. Add turkey, celery, green pepper, and onion together. Sautee until turkey is cooked.
5. Add the rest of the ingredients (excluding the toppings), bring to a boil then turn the heat down, cover and let simmer for a minimum of 35-40 minutes. You may have to add another cup or two of chicken broth.
6. Serve with optional avocado, Greek yogurt, or cheddar cheese.

Chapter Four Pork, beef & lamb

50. Pulled Pork BBQ

TIME TO PREPARE
5

COOK TIME
25

SERVING
4

PREPARED BY
NINJA FOODI

INGREDIENTS

1 lb. Pork Tenderloin
1 Tbsp Olive Oil
1/2 Tbsp Paprika
1/2 Tbsp Dry Mustard
1 tsp Kosher Salt
1 tsp Black Pepper
1/2 tsp Cumin
1 Tbsp Swerve Brown (or brown sugar)
3/4 C (180mL) Low Sodium Chicken Broth
3/4 C (192g) BBQ Sauce, divided
2 Tbsp (30g) Hot Sauce (optional)

STEPS TO COOK

Cooking the Pork Tenderloin

1. Mix the salt, pepper, paprika, dry mustard, cumin, and brown sugar together in a small bowl. Mix the chicken broth, 1/4 C (64g) bbq sauce, and optional hot sauce in another bowl. Set aside.
2. Rub or brush the olive oil on the pork tenderloin. Coat both sides of the pork tenderloin with the mixed spices.
3. Turn the Foodi's sauté function on its HI setting. Once the pot is hot (sizzles with a flick of water), add the pork tenderloin and cook for 2 minutes to develop a good sear on one side. Flip and cook for another 2 minutes. Add the broth mixture, seal the Foodi, and pressure cook on HI for 10-12* minutes with quick release pressure.
4. Transfer the cooked pork tenderloin to a large bowl to rest.

Shredding, Saucing, and Crisping

1. Turn the Foodi's sauté function on HI again until the remaining liquid has thickened to a sauce that leaves a trail when you drag a spatula across the pot, about 5-6 minutes.
2. Shred the pork tenderloin with two forks, meat claws, or stand mixer with a paddle attachment. Pour the remaining 1/2 C (128g) of BBQ sauce and stir before adding back to the Foodi with the thickened sauce. Stir to fully coat the pulled pork in the sauces.

51. Juicy Grilled Pork Chops

TIME TO PREPARE
10

COOK TIME
28

SERVING
4

PREPARED BY
Ninja foodi

INGREDIENTS	STEPS TO COOK
4 Pork Chops, bone in or boneless Pork Marinade	1. Make the pork marinade in advance and get your pork chops marinating in the refrigerator before cooking. 2. Insert removable cooking pot. Insert grill grate into your pot. 3. Press grill button, set to high (500 degrees), set time to 15 minutes. 4. Once "Add Food" flashes, add pork chops onto grill, close lid. And grill for 7-8 minutes, then flip the meat, closing grill once again. Cook for another 5 minutes and check internal temperature to see if has reached an internal temperature of 150 degrees. 5. Allow meat to rest 5 minutes before cutting and serving.

52. Foodi Buttery Ranch Pork Chops

TIME TO PREPARE
6

COOK TIME
12

SERVING
4

PREPARED BY
Ninja foodi

INGREDIENTS

8 pork chops
1/3 c butter
1 cup chicken broth
1 packet Hidden Valley Ranch Dressing
as desired, salt and pepper
1 tbsp cornstarch
2 tbsp water
1/4 cup sour cream (optional)

STEPS TO COOK

1. Wash and pat dry the pork chops.
2. Season with salt and pepper
3. Turn the Foodi onto 'sauté' and add 1 tbsp butter to melt.
4. Sauté the chops 3 - 4 minutes per side until they have a nice golden caramelization on each side.
5. Add the chicken broth in the bottom of the bowl
6. Sprinkle the ranch seasoning over the chops
7. Dot the butter in various places over and around the chops.
8. Manual pressure on high for 10 minutes. Be sure to turn the toggle on the pressure lid to 'sealing'
9. When time is complete, Do a natural release for 15 minutes. QR the rest of the pressure after time is up. Carefully remove the lid after the silver pin drops.
10. Remove the chops and tent with foil to keep warm. Make the slurry of cornstarch and water, and pour it into the Foodi bowl. Turn the machine onto Sauté.
11. Add the sour cream now, if you are including it in the recipe. Stir until the sauce thickens.
12. Place chops back into the sauce for a minute or two and then serve them over rice or potatoes, etc. Enjoy!

53. Pork Tacos

TIME TO PREPARE
10

COOK TIME
40

SERVING
12

PREPARED BY
Ninja foodi

INGREDIENTS	STEPS TO COOK
Pork tenderloin (2-3 lbs.) 1 Tbsp coconut palm sugar 2 tsp Paprika 2 tsp Garlic Powder 1/2 tsp Cumin 2 tsp Onion Powder 1/8 tsp cayenne 1/3 cup Apple Cider Vinegar 1 1/4 cup broth Siete Grain Free Taco Shells Mango Salsa	1. Cut pork tenderloin into chunks 2. Mix dry ingredients 3. Season pork with let ingredients and let sit 1-2 hours' min (or overnight) 4. Set Ninja Foodi to sear/sauté and slightly brown tenderloin chunks on all sides 5. Remove pork from Foodi and add liquid 6. Deglaze bottom of Foodi 7. Add pork back to the Foodi 8. Attach pressure cook lid 9. Set Ninja Foodi to Pressure Cook on High 10. Cook for 35 minutes 11. Allow Foodi to slow release for up to 5 minutes then quick release pressure. DO NOT remove lid until pressure is fully released. 12. Shred pork with fork 13. Prepare your tacos and serve with your favorite toppings.

54. Crispy Pork Carnitas

TIME TO PREPARE
10

COOK TIME
45

SERVING
4

PREPARED BY
NINJA FOODI

INGREDIENTS

- 2 lbs. pork butt chopped into 2-inch pieces
- 1 tsp kosher salt
- 1/2 tsp oregano
- 1/2 tsp cumin
- 1 orange cut in half
- 1 onion peeled and cut in half
- 6 garlic cloves peeled and crushed
- 1/2 cup chicken broth

STEPS TO COOK

1. Place pork, salt, oregano, and cumin in Ninja Foodi pressure cook insert. Combine making sure the seasonings are covering the pork.
2. Take the orange and squeeze the juices over the pork. Put the squeezed orange in the insert, along with the onion, garlic cloves, and ½ cup chicken broth.
3. Cover the Ninja Foodi with the pressure cooker cover, ensuring the valve is set to seal. Setting up the Ninja Foodi to High Pressure and cook for 20 minutes.
4. Once the 20-minute timer is complete, do a quick release by switching the valve to vent. Once all the pressure is released, open the lid and remove the orange, onion, and garlic cloves.
5. Set the Ninja Foodi to sauté and select md:hi. The liquid will begin to simmer. Allow the liquid to cook until it reduces, about 10-15 minutes.
6. Once the majority of the liquid has reduced, press stop on the Ninja Foodi and then close the Ninja Foodi Air Crisp lid.
7. Select Broil and adjust the time to 8 minutes.
8. Once complete, use the crispy delicious meat in tacos, bowls, sandwiches, wraps, etc. Top with cilantro or any of your favorite toppings.

55. Pork Chops

TIME TO PREPARE	COOK TIME	SERVING	PREPARED BY
10	12	4	NINJA FOODI

INGREDIENTS

- 4 pork chops
- 8 strips bacon
- 1/2 c brown sugar
- 1 tbsp salt
- 1 tbsp garlic salt
- 1/2 tbsp chili powder makes it mild/medium heat
- 1/2 tbsp paprika

STEPS TO COOK

1. Preheat air fryer to 400 degrees while you're preparing all of this. Mix seasonings and pour on to a plate. Lay 1 pork chop on seasoning, flip, cover and coat both sides.
2. Lay 2 slices of bacon down horizontally, use a cutting board for this. Wrap the top portion of the pork chop (meaty end) and fasten with 2 toothpicks so bacon stays on. Insert vertically so it is not sticking out and chop can lay flat.
3. Spray inside of air fryer basket with non-stick spray.
4. Lay 2-3 pork chops inside the basket, as many as you can without overlapping. We can only fit 2.
5. Close lid and air fry for a total of 10 minutes (approx., time varies according to how thick your pieces are), flipping halfway through the cooking process.
6. Remove and check internal temperature to ensure they're done. Let it rest for at least 5 minutes before cutting. Remove toothpicks before eating

56. Herb Crusted Pork Chops

TIME TO PREPARE
20

SERVING
4

COOK TIME
16

PREPARED BY
Ninja foodi

INGREDIENTS	STEPS TO COOK
4 thick cut pork chops 2 tsp sage 2 tsp thyme 2 tsp oregano 1 tsp rosemary 1 tsp paprika 1 tsp garlic powder 1 tsp salt 1/2 tsp black pepper	1. Combine the sage, thyme, oregano, rosemary, paprika, garlic powder, salt, and black pepper. Set aside. 2. Preheat your Air Fryer to 360 degrees Fahrenheit. 3. While you Air Fryer is preheating, rub a little bit of olive oil over the pork chops and sprinkle the herb mixture over the chops, covering all sides. 4. Place in Air Fryer basket making sure the chops don't overlap. 5. Cook on 360 degrees for 14-16 minutes, flipping halfway. Pork chops are done when they have reached an internal temperature of 145 degrees Fahrenheit. 6. Remove pork chops from the Air Fryer and loosely cover with foil. Allow them to rest for about 5 minutes.

57. BBQ Pork

TIME TO PREPARE
70

COOK TIME
45

SERVING
6

PREPARED BY
NINJA FOODI

INGREDIENTS

1 lb./500g Pork shoulder, sliced 2" thick
1 cup Water
6 Scallion stalks

MARINADE
3 tbsp Garlic (minced)
1 Onion (diced)
1/2 cup Ketchup
2 tbsp Soy sauce
1 tbsp Salt
1 tbsp Hoisin sauce
1/4 cup Honey
1 tbsp Five-spice powder
1 cup Sugar
1 tbsp Olive Oil

STEPS TO COOK

1. Combine the diced onion, garlic, ketchup, hoisin sauce, soy sauce, honey, five-spice, sugar and oil into a large mixing bowl
2. Add the pork shoulder to the marinade and marinate in the refrigerator for 1 hour
3. Pour 1 cup of water into the Ninja Foodi inner pot and add in the scallion stalks
4. Place the marinated pork into the inner pot on the reversible rack set in low position
5. Place the pressure lid and set the release valve to "SEAL"
6. Pressure cook on HIGH for 35 minutes
7. Flip the release valve to "VENT" to manually release pressure
8. Remove the pork and place it back into the remaining marinade
9. Add 1 cup of sugar onto a plate and sugarcoat the pork by dipping both sides into the sugar
10. Line the bottom of the inner pot with foil to prevent excessive smoking from any marinade that falls to the bottom of the pot
11. Layer the pork in the Cook & Crisp Basket using the Cook & Crisp insert rack
12. Bake at 400ºF for 10 minutes or until it reaches desired doneness.

58. Beef and Cabbage

TIME TO PREPARE
10

COOK TIME
1H 20 MIN

SERVING
8

PREPARED BY
NINJA FOODI

INGREDIENTS

3 lbs. cabbage
4 lbs. corned beef with seasoning packet
1/4 cup balsamic vinegar
1 cup water beer will work too
2 lbs. carrots
2 1/2 lbs. potatoes Yukon Gold are preferred

Brown Sugar Glaze
1/4 cup brown sugar
1/4 cup balsamic vinegar
1 Tbsp mustard country style grey poupon

Extra Seasoning Blend
1 Bay Leaf
1 Tbsp peppercorn whole
1 Tbsp mustard seed whole

STEPS TO COOK

1. Cut the cabbage in to 8 sections. See post for more details. Add 1 cup of water and 1/4 cup balsamic vinegar to the inner pot. Place the cabbage sections on the bottom of the inner pot. Add in the extra seasoning blend as well as the packet of seasonings that comes with the corned beef.
2. Place the corned beef fat side up on top of the cabbage. Put the pressure lid on and set the Ninja Foodi to high pressure for 7 minutes. When the time is up, immediate release the pressure.
3. Remove the corned beef and set on a cutting board. Remove the cabbage and put in a bowl. Place the rack in the low position into the inner pot and place the corned beef on the rack, fat side up. Put the pressure lid back on and set the Ninja Foodi to high pressure for 45 minutes. When the time is up, allow to natural release for 10 minutes. Remove the rack with the corned beef out and set to the side.
4. Peel and cut carrots into thirds. Cut potatoes into quarters. See post for details. Place the carrots into the bottom of the Ninja Foodi and place the potatoes on top. Set the corned beef on top of the potatoes and put the pressure lid on. Set the pressure to high and cook for 2 minutes. All the Ninja Foodi to naturally release its pressure for 10 minutes.
5. Make the glaze: combine the 1/4 cup of balsamic vinegar, brown sugar, and mustard in a small bowl.
6. Remove the corned beef and set to the side. Remove the carrots and potatoes and place in a large mixing

bowl. Pour the juice from the inner pot into the bowl to keep the carrots and potatoes warm.

7. Place the cabbage around the sides of the fry basket. Place the corned beef in the center. Pour the glaze over the top. Set the Air Crisp function to 400° F and Air Crisp for 20-25 minutes. Remove beef and set on a cutting board to rest for 15 minutes.
8. Move the cabbage around a bit and add in potatoes and carrots to the air fry basket. Air Crisp on 400° F for 15 minutes.
9. Slice the corned beef against the grain. See video for more details. Serve with cabbage, potatoes, and carrots. Enjoy!

59. Ninja Foodi Picadillo

TIME TO PREPARE
5

COOK TIME
30

SERVING
10

PREPARED BY
Ninja foodi

INGREDIENTS

Sauté
2 lbs. Ground Beef (96/4)
2 Tbsp (32g) Olive Oil
1 (250g) Yellow Onion, diced
1 (150g) Green Bell Pepper, diced
4 cloves Garlic, minced

For Pressure Cooking
1 C (240mL) Beef Broth
8 oz. can Tomato Sauce
6 oz. can Tomato Paste
1/4 C (60g) White Wine Vinegar*
10 Jalapeño Stuffed Olives, roughly chopped
2 oz. Raisins
1/2 Tbsp Cumin
1 tsp Dried Oregano
Salt and Pepper, to taste

STEPS TO COOK

1. Set the Foodi's sauté function to HI while you prep the vegetables.
2. Add the olive oil to the Foodi pot. Once hot, add the onion and bell pepper. Cook until soft, about 6-8 minutes. Add the garlic and cook for another 30-60 seconds until fragrant. Put the ground beef and cook until no pink remains.
3. Add the pressure-cooking ingredients and stir well. Seal and pressure cook on HI for 6-8 minutes** with quick release pressure (vent as soon as the Foodi's cook cycle is finished). Optional: Stir in 1-2 Tbsp of chopped cilantro after the Picadillo is finished cooking.

60. BBQ Beef Short Ribs

TIME TO PREPARE
15

COOK TIME
40

SERVING
2

PREPARED BY
Ninja foodi

INGREDIENTS

2 Beef Short Ribs (see notes)
1/4 c Red Wine
3/4 c Beef Stock
1/4 c Diced Onion
1/2 c bbq sauce
Seasoning as desired:
Seasoning salt
Garlic Powder
Onion Powder
1 Tbsp Cornstarch (see notes)

STEPS TO COOK

1. Season the beef ribs with the seasonings above, to your preference.
2. Add the onion, wine, and broth to the bottom of the Foodi cooking bowl
3. Close the toggle switch to sealing
4. Pressure cook on manual, high, for 40 minutes.
5. Do a natural release for 10 minutes, and then carefully release any remaining pressure until the pin drops and it's safe to open the lid.
6. Remove the ribs to a plate.
7. Generously brush the bbq sauce over the entire surface of the ribs. Place the ribs back into the pot, on the top rack of the air crisping rack.
8. Air crisp the ribs for 10 minutes, watching them closely so as not to burn. Feel free to flip them halfway through.
9. Remove the ribs to rest and take out the rack.
10. Mix up the slurry and pour into the pan juices in the pot to thicken.
11. Spoon over the ribs and enjoy!

61. Sesame Beef

TIME TO PREPARE
10

COOK TIME
12

SERVING
2

PREPARED BY NINJA FOODI

INGREDIENTS

Stir Fry:
1 pound of flank steak, cut into strips
1/2 cup snow peas
1/2 cup shredded carrots
1/2 cup broccoli
1/2 cup sliced red onions

Beef Marinade:
¼ cup of hoisin sauce
2 teaspoons of minced garlic
1 teaspoon of sesame oil
1 tablespoon of soy sauce
1 teaspoon of ground ginger
¼ cup of water
Stir Fry Oil (or sesame oil)

STEPS TO COOK

1. Start by plugging in the air fryer, and then press the start button, and then hit the grill. It will need to preheat.
2. When the display reads Add Food that means that the air fry is ready for you to add the food.
3. Add the Stir Fry Oil, and then wait about 30 seconds.
4. Add the beef, vegetables, and sauce to the air fryer, and then close the lid and set the timer for 10 minutes. But about every 3 minutes, use tongs to flip the meat, otherwise, it will stick to the grate.
5. Plate, serve and enjoy!

62. Roast Beef

TIME TO PREPARE
15

COOK TIME
50

SERVING
2

PREPARED BY NINJA FOODI

INGREDIENTS

2-pound Top Round Roast
Rub
1.33 Tbsp sea salt
1.33 Tbsp pepper course
1.67 tsp onion powder
1.67 tsp garlic powder

STEPS TO COOK

1. Allow your roast to come to room temp. This takes about 1 hour.
2. Combine the rub ingredients and generously apply to the outside of the meat.
3. Preheat the Ninja Foodi on Broil with the rack in the low position inside the inner pot for 10 minutes.
4. Broil the roast beef on the rack in the low position for 25 minutes. Turn the Ninja Foodi off and keep the lid closed for 25 minutes. See notes if you want your meat cooked to a different temperature.
5. Remove and allow to rest for 10 minutes. Slice thinly against the grain.
6. Serve & Enjoy!

63. Beef and Broccoli

TIME TO PREPARE
15

COOK TIME
10

SERVING
5

PREPARED BY
Ninja foodi

INGREDIENTS

1 lb. flank steak sliced thin
1 tsp ginger minced or fresh and grated
2 tsp minced garlic
2 tsp olive oil
1/2 c soy sauce
1/2 c beef broth or water
1/4 c rice wine vinegar
2 tbsp brown sugar
1 bag broccoli frozen, florets, 10 oz.
2 tbsp cornstarch dissolved into 1/4 c water

STEPS TO COOK

1. Place steak, ginger, garlic, and oil into the bottom of your pressure cooker.
2. Turn Instant Pot or Ninja foodi on sauté, use brown/sear on Crock Pot Express. Cook until the meat is no longer pink. Turn pot off.
3. Stir in soy sauce, broth, vinegar and brown sugar.
4. Close lid and steam valve and set to pressure high for 5 minutes.
5. Do a quick release and lift lid.
6. Add frozen broccoli into your pot and set to sauté again (with lid open).
7. For Crock Pot express use sear/brown button for this step.
8. Stir slowly until broccoli is cooked.
9. In a small bowl whisk together cornstarch and about 5 tbsp of hot liquid from pot until mixture is smooth.
10. Turn pot off.
11. Serve alone or on a bed of rice!

64. Beef Taco Soup

TIME TO PREPARE
10

COOK TIME
4

SERVING
6

PREPARED BY
NINJA FOODI

INGREDIENTS

1 lb. Lean Ground Beef

1 Packet of Taco Seasoning Mix or Gluten-Free Taco Seasoning Mix

1 15oz Can of Black Beans, Drained

1 14.5oz Can have Diced Tomatoes

1 14.5oz Can of Beef Broth

1 Cup Corn

1 Cup Water

1/3 Chopped Hatch Chiles

STEPS TO COOK

1. Begin by browning the ground beef. If you are using a Ninja Foodi or Instant Pot, this can be done right in the pot by sautéing on high.
2. Once the meat is browned, add in the taco seasoning per the package instructions.
3. Add in the black beans, tomatoes, broth, corn, and water.
4. Stir in the chiles.
5. Set to manual high pressure for 4 minutes.
6. Once it comes to pressure, quick release and serve with sides of your choice such as Doritos, Corn Chips, Shredded Cheese, or Sour Cream.

65. Beef Stroganoff

TIME TO PREPARE
5

COOK TIME
15

SERVING
6

PREPARED BY
Ninja foodi

INGREDIENTS

2 tablespoons oil- vegetable or canola
Beef stew 1 kilo of meat cut into 1-inch cubes
1 cup diced white onion
1 1/2 teaspoon salt
1 teaspoon pepper
2 tablespoons flour
2 cups beef broth
2 tablespoons Worcestershire sauce
2 tablespoons soy sauce
2 tablespoons minced garlic
3 cups sliced mushrooms
½ cup sour cream
8 oz. wide egg noodles (1/2 package for this recipe)

STEPS TO COOK

1. Turn on your Ninja Foodi and select the sauté function
2. Add oil and heat for 1 minute
3. Add onion and cook until the onion becomes tender and translucent
4. Add beef and season with 1 teaspoon salt and 1 teaspoon pepper
5. Brown beef on all sides- stir frequently
6. Add garlic
7. Add Worcestershire sauce and soy sauce
8. Stir in mushrooms
9. Stir in flour being sure to coat the meat and mushrooms evenly
10. Pour in beef broth and ½ teaspoon salt
11. Close the pressure cooker lid and set on high pressure for 10 minutes with the vent on "seal"
12. When timer beeps, turn nozzle to "vent" and quick release all pressure
13. Open lid and add in egg noodles
14. Close the lid and set on high pressure for 5 minutes with the vent on "seal"
15. When the timer beeps, allow pressure to naturally release for 5 minutes
16. Open lid and add in ½ cup of sour cream.
17. Stir and serve!

66. Cheesy Beef and Rice Casserole

TIME TO PREPARE 10   **COOK TIME** 20   **SERVING** 8   **PREPARED BY NINJA FOODI**

INGREDIENTS

- 1/2 cup onions chopped
- 1/2 cup red bell pepper chopped
- 1/4 cup scallions chopped
- 2 cloves garlic chopped
- 1 and 1/2 cup frozen chopped spinach
- 3 cups rice
- 3 and 1/3 cups chicken broth you can substitute beef broth or water
- 1- and 1/2-pounds lean ground beef
- 1 cup shredded cheddar cheese
- 1/4 cup shredded mozzarella cheese OPTIONAL
- 2 tablespoons canola or vegetable oil
- 1 teaspoon kosher salt
- 1/2 teaspoon ground pepper
- 1/2 teaspoon granulated garlic
- 1/2 teaspoon paprika

STEPS TO COOK

1. Set the Ninja Foodi to SAUTE and add oil
2. add the chopped onion, pepper and green onion to the Foodi and sauté for 5 minutes
3. add ground beef, salt, pepper, garlic powder and paprika then brown for 5 minutes then add garlic. Cook for 30 seconds more
4. Stir in the rice then add chicken broth and frozen spinach
5. Cover the Ninja Foodi with the pressure cook lid then cook on HIGH pressure for 3 minutes
6. Natural release for 10 minutes then manually releases the rest of the pressure
7. Reserve 1/2 a cup of cheese for the top. Stir in the rest of the cheddar and mozzarella cheese.
8. Top with reserved cheddar cheese then close the AIR CRISP LID. BROIL for about 5 minutes or until the cheese is melted and browned.

67. Beef with Rice

TIME TO PREPARE
10

COOK TIME
20

SERVING
8

PREPARED BY NINJA FOODI

INGREDIENTS

1-pound beef stew meat
1/2 cup diced onion
1 tablespoon garlic
14.5-ounce tomatoes (Canned- I used garlic and olive oil petite diced)
8-ounce mushrooms (sliced)
ounce can beef gravy
2 teaspoons salt
2 teaspoons pepper
1 tablespoon olive oil
1 cup beef broth
1 cup white rice (uncooked)

STEPS TO COOK

1. Turn Ninja Foodi on sauté
2. Once the pot is hot, add oil
3. Add beef and season with salt and pepper
4. Sauté beef until browned on all sides
5. Move the beef over to half of the pot and add onions to the other half of the pot
6. Sauté onions until tender- a little browning will add some great flavor!
7. Stir beef and onions together and add garlic
8. Add tomatoes, mushrooms, beef broth and canned gravy
9. Stir and close lid
10. Cook on high pressure with valve set to "seal" for 20 minutes
11. Once timer beeps, let pressure release naturally for 10 minutes
12. Quick release remaining pressure and then open lid and stir
13. Pour in uncooked white rice
14. Close pressure-cooking lid and move valve to "seal" position. Cook on high pressure for 4 minutes.
15. When timer beeps, naturally release pressure for 5 minutes and then quick release any remaining pressure.
16. Open lid and stir

68. Beef Stew

TIME TO PREPARE
10

COOK TIME
15

SERVING
4

PREPARED BY
NINJA FOODI

INGREDIENTS

1.33 lbs. stew meat diced small
1 c onion diced
1.33 pkg. brown gravy mix dry
0.67 c frozen peas and carrots
0.67 c beef broth or water
0.67 tsp olive oil
salt and pepper

STEPS TO COOK

1. Set pot to sauté and add olive oil. Season meat with salt and pepper and add in stew meat + onions, brown beef until no longer pink on the outside. Turn pot off.
2. Add 1/2 c. of your broth. Put on pressure cooker lid and set to high pressure for 15 minutes followed by a quick release.
3. Remove lid and add frozen peas and carrots. Stir and set to sauté mode again.
4. Whisk together in a bowl your remaining broth and 1 packet of dry gravy mix, add this into the pot and allow to bubble and thicken.
5. Then I like it thicker so I add a 2nd packet of gravy mix. Stir this in allowing it to continue to thicken as much as you desire. Turn pot off and season with salt and pepper to taste.
6. Serve over mashed potatoes or in a bowl with rolls on the side.

69. Lamb Shanks with Roasted Carrots

TIME TO PREPARE
10

COOK TIME
55

SERVING
4

PREPARED BY
NINJA FOODI

INGREDIENTS

3 tablespoons olive oil, divided

4 lamb shanks (about 3 pounds' total)

2 teaspoons kosher salt, plus more for seasoning

2 teaspoons paprika

1 teaspoon ground cumin

1 teaspoon ground cinnamon

1 teaspoon ground black pepper

1 cup red wine

2 cloves garlic, peeled

1-pound baby carrots

1 tablespoon instant flour

STEPS TO COOK

1. Add 2 tablespoons olive oil to the pot. Select SEAR/SAUTÉ and set to HIGH. Select START/STOP to begin. Allow to preheat for 5 minutes.
2. After 5 minutes, add lamb shanks to pot. Sear until browned on all sides, about 10 minutes.
3. Add salt and spices to the pot and cook until aromatic, stirring, about one minute.
4. Add the red wine and garlic to the pot. Scrape the bottom for any browned bits. Mount the pressure cover, making sure that the pressure release valve is in the SEAL position.
5. Select PRESSURE and set to HIGH. Set time to 15 minutes. Select START/STOP to begin.
6. When pressure cooking is complete, quick release the pressure by moving the pressure release valve to the VENT position.
7. Place the reversible rack in the pot over shanks, making sure rack is in the higher position. Place carrots on rack.
8. Select PRESSURE and set to HIGH. Set time to 10 minutes. Select START/STOP to begin.
9. When pressure cooking is complete, quick release the pressure by moving the pressure release valve to the VENT position.
10. Drizzle 1 tablespoon olive oil over the carrots. Select BROIL and set time to 10 minutes. Select START/STOP to begin.
11. When cooking is complete, remove carrots and lamb shanks from the pot and allow to rest.
12. Select SEAR/SAUTÉ and set to HIGH. Select START/STOP to begin. Add instant flour to the liquid in the pot, whisking constantly. Bring mixture to a boil. Once boiling, press the Power button to turn off SEAR/SAUTÉ. Ladle the sauce over the lamb and serve.

70. Tomato Fresca Lamb Chops

TIME TO PREPARE
6

COOK TIME
12

SERVING
4

PREPARED BY
NINJA FOODI

INGREDIENTS

2 large ripe tomatoes, cored & quartered,
3 cloves garlic, peeled,
1/2 yellow onion, peeled,
3 tbsp. fresh oregano leaves,
2 tbsps. olive oil,
4 lamb chops, pounded flat, seasoned with salt & pepper,
1 cup white wine

STEPS TO COOK

1. Place tomatoes, garlic, onion & oregano into the Single Serve Cup. Pulse the Single Serve button until semi-smooth.
2. Remove the blades from the cup after blending & set aside.
3. In a large non-stick sauté pan, heat the oil on medium-high heat. Put lamb chops & sear 3 minutes per side, until golden brown. Remove chops from pan to a plate & set aside.
4. Stir wine into pan to deglaze. Reduce heat to medium, stir in tomato sauce & simmer until heated through.
5. Return chops & juices to pan, gently stirring into sauce & simmer for 2 to 4 minutes. Serve chops with sauce spooned over top.
6. Go ahead, embrace your inner meal prepper.

71. Rack of Lamb Kebabs

TIME TO PREPARE	COOK TIME	SERVING	PREPARED BY
30	10	4	NINJA FOODI

INGREDIENTS

- 500g hand cut rack of lamb
- 1 large onion
- 4 tbsp garlic paste
- 3 cloves
- 2-star anise
- 100ml water
- 1 tbsp chili powder
- 1/2 tbsp turmeric powder
- 1 tbsp garam masala
- 1 tbsp ginger paste
- 1 tbsp garlic paste
- 1 tbsp sunflower oil

STEPS TO COOK

1. Cut the large onion coarsely and blitz in a food processor. In the Ninja Foodi pot mix the blitzed onion, garlic paste, cloves, star anise and water together with the lamb
2. Assemble the pressure cooker lid, making sure the valve is in the seal position
3. Select PRESSURE and set to HIGH. Set the time to 5 minutes. Select START/PAUSE to begin. When the pressure cooking is complete, quick release by moving the valve to the vent position
4. Remove the lamb from the cooked liquid and dry them with a kitchen towel
5. In a small bowl mix together the chili powder, turmeric powder, garam masala, ginger and garlic paste into a thick paste. Gently coat the dried lamb racks with the paste
6. Set the Foodi to Air Crisp at 200c, place the lamb racks on to the reversible rack and drizzle a tbsp of oil on it. Air crisp this for 10 minutes and VOILA! They are ready.
7. Serve with a yogurt and mint dip (Greek yogurt + mint sauce) – quick and easy

72. Broiling Steak

TIME TO PREPARE
11

COOK TIME
5

SERVING
4

PREPARED BY
NINJA FOODI

INGREDIENTS

4 Medium Cut Ribeye Steaks
Steak Seasoning to taste

STEPS TO COOK

1. Season steaks and let sit on kitchen counter for 30 minutes to bring closer to room temperature.
2. Preheat Ninja Foodi with broiling/steaming rack set in highest position by using the broil feature for 5 minutes.
3. Carefully place steaks on the racks (they should sizzle) and broil for 5-7 minutes depending on how you like your steak (see notes).
4. Flip steaks and broil for another 5-7 minutes.
5. Remove steaks from the Ninja Foodi and allow to rest on a cutting board for 5 minutes before cutting into the steak.

73. Lamb Shanks

TIME TO PREPARE
1H 20 MIN

COOK TIME
2 H

SERVING
6

PREPARED BY
NINJA FOODI

INGREDIENTS

- 3 lamb shanks preferably skinless
- 1/2 cup olive oil divided
- 1 green chili pepper sliced
- 3 cloves garlic minced
- 1 Tbsp. smoked paprika
- 1 Tbsp. oregano
- 2 tsp. salt
- 1/4 tsp. ground cumin
- 2 Tbsp. brown sugar
- 1 cinnamon stick
- 1 medium onion roughly chopped
- 3 medium carrots roughly chopped
- 2 bay leaves
- 2 cups red wine
- 4 cups beef stock
- 3 Tbsp. corn starch
- 1/4 cup water

STEPS TO COOK

1. In large bowl - combine lamb, pepper, garlic, paprika, oregano, salt, cumin, brown sugar, cinnamon sticks, and 1/4 cup oil. Mix up well to coat meat, then marinate from 30 minutes to overnight.
2. Using sauté setting. When is hot add 1/4 cup olive oil and thoroughly brown lamb on all sides – making sure to render all the fat. Once browned, remove lamb shanks and set aside.
3. Add onions, carrots, bay leaves, and remaining marinade to the foodi. Sauté until onions become translucent – about 5 minutes.
4. Add red wine to deglaze the pot - making sure to scrape all the bits stuck to the bottom. Return lamb to pot. Simmer to reduce by half - about 10 minutes.
5. Add stock. Cook for 30 minutes at high pressure.
6. Once cook time is complete, allow pressure naturally release. Remove shanks and set aside.
7. Pour the liquid through a fine mesh strainer and return to the pan. Discard cooked ingredients. Separately in a small bowl, combine cornstarch and water, then add to pot.
8. Switch the ninja foodi back to sauté setting and simmer until sauce reaches desired thickness. Return the lamb to the pan and leave to rest in the sauce until ready to serve.
9. Serve lamb with polenta or mashed potatoes topped with gravy!

74. Braised Lamb Shanks with Red Wine

TIME TO PREPARE
20

COOK TIME
1H 30 MIN

SERVING
4

PREPARED BY
NINJA FOODI

INGREDIENTS

4 Lamb Shanks
2 Tablespoon Extra Virgin Olive Oil
6 sprigs Rosemary
2 cups red wine for cooking I rely on Rex Goliath Pinot Noir
1 cup prunes diced
1/2 cup carrots diced
4 garlic cloves crushed
Salt & Pepper to taste

STEPS TO COOK

1. Preheat oven to 350
2. In a Dutch Oven heat EVOO on med hi heat
3. Season shank with salt & pepper
4. Working in batches of 2 shanks brown shanks on all sides
5. Remove shanks to cutting board
6. Reduce heat to medium add in prunes, carrots & garlic, brown about 3 minutes
7. Pour in red wine de-glazing the pan (run a heat proof spatula or wooden spoon along the bottom of the pan to get up the crispiest)
8. Add in the lamb shanks
9. Rest Rosemary on lamb shank cover and place in oven
10. Cook for 60-90 min. Lamb shanks size are dependent on the lamb if smaller they will cook faster. If it is not place back in stove and check in another 15 minutes. Lamb shanks take abuse of heat easily so do not fret if you are new to this.
11. Rest for 5 minutes before serving.

75. Lamb with Mint

TIME TO PREPARE 55   **COOK TIME** 45   **SERVING** 6   **PREPARED BY NINJA FOODI**

INGREDIENTS

- 1 half leg of lamb (raw) approximately 1.2 kg
- 3 cloves of garlic (optional), peeled and thinly sliced
- 1 small bunch fresh mint (approximately 25g), finely sliced
- 20ml rapeseed/vegetable oil
- Salt and freshly ground black pepper
- 25g thickening gravy granules

STEPS TO COOK

1. Place the lamb on a suitable board (for meat). If using garlic, puncture the flesh all around (around 30 times) with the tip of a sharp knife to make short slits in the meat
2. Place a slither of sliced garlic into each slit and season the lamb with salt and freshly ground black pepper
3. Pour 200mls of cold water into the pot of your Ninja Foodi
4. Place the lamb into the Cook & Crisp Basket and place the basket into the pot (You may have to trim the bone if it is too long for the basket)
5. Assemble the pressure lid, making sure the pressure release valve is in the SEAL position. Select PRESSURE and set to HIGH. Set time to 32 minutes. Select START/STOP to begin
6. When pressure cooking is complete, allow pressure to naturally release for 2 minutes. After 2 minutes, quick release the remaining pressure by carefully moving the pressure release to the VENT position. Remove the lid when unit has finished releasing pressure
7. Brush the lamb with the rapeseed/vegetable oil
8. Close the crisping lid. Select AIR CRISP, setting the temperature to 200°C and set time to 8 minutes. Select START/STOP to begin. When cooking is complete, remove the basket from the pot and leave to rest on a plate, covering loosely with aluminum foil

9. To make a sauce, add the gravy granules to the pot containing the cooking liquid and stir with a plastic whisk to mix in (or spoon). A little more water, stock or even a drop of wine can be added at this point if desired. Assemble the pressure lid, making sure the pressure release vale is in the SEAL position.
10. Select PRESSURE and set to LOW. Set time to 3 minutes. Select START/STOP to begin
11. When pressure cooking is complete, quick release the pressure by moving the pressure release to the VENT position. Carefully remove the lid once the pressure has been released
12. Stir the sauce and adjust the consistency with a little more liquid (water, stock or wine) if it is too thick. Pass the sauce through a sieve into a saucepan or sauce-boat and add the finely sliced fresh mint
13. To serve, carve the rested lamb and place onto a warm serving plate. Coat with sauce and serve with potatoes (such as dauphin Oise) and freshly steamed seasonal vegetables

76. Steak and Vegetable Bowls

TIME TO PREPARE
5

COOK TIME
15

SERVING
6

PREPARED BY
Ninja foodi

INGREDIENTS

2 KC Strip Steaks
1 Cup Red Bell Pepper, Diced
1 Cup Green Bell Pepper, Diced
1 Cup Yellow Squash, Diced
1 Cup Mushroom, Sliced
1/4 Cup White Onion, Diced
1/2 Tbsp Steak Seasoning
Olive Oil Cooking Spray

STEPS TO COOK

1. Cut the steak into smaller cubed chunks.
2. Spray the basket of the air fryer or ninja Foodi basket.
3. Place the steaks and vegetables in the air fryer or ninja Foodi basket.
4. Sprinkle evenly with the seasoning.
5. Spray with olive oil spray.
6. Cook for 7 minutes on 390 degrees.
7. Carefully open the lid and stir and mix the ingredients, coat with additional olive oil spray.
8. Cook for an additional 8 minutes at 390 degrees or until done to your preference.

77. Prime Rib in the Ninja Foodi

TIME TO PREPARE
5

COOK TIME
45

SERVING
6

PREPARED BY
NINJA FOODI

INGREDIENTS

3-pound prime rib roast
6-8 cloves garlic
1 Tbsp Sea Salt fine grind
½ Tbsp pepper fresh cracked or coarse grind
3 sprigs Rosemary
½ onion sliced

STEPS TO COOK

1. Allow the prime rib to sit at room temp for about 2 hours to take the chill off. Heat the Ninja Foodi on broil for 10 minutes.
2. Cut 6-8 slits in the fat cap on top about ½-1" deep and insert a garlic clove into each one. The garlic should not be sticking out too much.
3. Place sprigs of Rosemary and onion slices on the reversible rack in the low position. Place the prime rib on top. Place the rack in the Ninja Foodi and broil for 5 minutes per pound. Don't open the lid.
4. After the Ninja Foodi goes through the cool cycle and without opening the lid, select the Bake/Roast function and set the time based on weight and how you like your prime rib cooked. See Notes. Check a temperature halfway through cooking and adjust time as needed.
5. Once the internal temperature is 5° less than the way you want it cooked, remove the rack with the prime rib and allow it to rest for 10-15 minutes. Serve & Enjoy!

78. Ninja Foodi Steak

TIME TO PREPARE
5

COOK TIME
17

SERVING
1

PREPARED BY
Ninja foodi

INGREDIENTS

filet mignon
avocado oil
Celtic sea salt
pepper

STEPS TO COOK

1. Lightly spray steak with oil
2. salt and pepper to taste
3. place your steak on high rack
4. select air crisp on ninja Foodi
5. set temp at 375
6. set time for 17 minutes
7. flip steak over at halfway point

Chapter Five Fish & Seafood

79. Ninja Foodi Crab Legs

TIME TO PREPARE
5

SERVING
4

COOK TIME
2

PREPARED BY
Ninja foodi

INGREDIENTS	STEPS TO COOK

Ingredients:

4 Crab Leg clusters
2 Tablespoons garlic-minced or chopped
1 Tablespoon Tony Chachere's seasoning
1 Cup water
1 Lemon-sliced

Steps:

1. How to make Ninja Foodi Crab Legs?
2. Place trivet in Ninja Foodi
3. Pour water into pot Add garlic to pot
4. Add Tony Chachere's seasoning
5. Place sliced lemons on trivet
6. Add crab legs to pot
7. Close lid and move valve to "seal" position
8. Cook on high for 2 minutes
9. When timer beeps move seal to "release" and quick release all pressure
10. When the pressure is released take off the lid Let Crab Legs continue to steam in the Ninja Foodi for up to 5 minutes
11. Serve with melted butter

80. Ninja Foodi Shrimp Boil

TIME TO PREPARE 10 | **COOK TIME** 5 | **SERVING** 6 | **PREPARED BY NINJA FOODI**

INGREDIENTS

- 1 lb. red potatoes cut in half
- 4 ears fresh corn snapped in half
- 12 oz. Cajun style andouille sausage cut into 2-inch pieces
- 4 cups water
- 1 1/2 Tbsp Zataran's shrimp boil liquid
- 3 tsp Old Bay seasoning divided
- 1 lb. fresh shrimp peeled and deveined
- 1 lb. fresh mussels
- fresh chopped parsley optional
- Lemon slices optional

Garlic Butter for Dipping
- 1/2 cup butter melted
- 1/2 tsp garlic powder

STEPS TO COOK

1. Add red potatoes, corn, sausage, water, shrimp boil liquid, and 2 tsp old bay to the Ninja Foodi insert and stir. Cook on high pressure for 4 minutes. Once timer is complete, do a quick release and open lid once all pressure is released.
2. Add shrimp and mussels and 1 tsp of old bay. Stir. Cover and cook on high pressure for 1 minute. When the timer turns off, wait for natural release for 2 minutes, then quickly release the remaining pressure.
3. Combine butter and garlic powder in a separate bowl and use as a dipping sauce.
4. Sprinkle with parsley and serve with lemon on the side. Enjoy

81. Cajun Shrimp Boil

 TIME TO PREPARE 15
 COOK TIME 2
 SERVING 8
 PREPARED BY NINJA FOODI

INGREDIENTS

2.67 onions quartered, I used Vidalia
4 ears of corn
8 Yukon gold potatoes
1.33 jalapeno pepper
1.33-2.67 red chili peppers dried
1.33 bulb garlic
2.67 cups chicken stock
18.67 ounces Andouille sausage
sprigs Thyme
1.33 lemon halved
2.67 lbs. shrimp large & frozen
1.33 zucchini

Whole Spice Seasoning Blend
1.33 Tbsp black peppercorns
0.67 Tbsp mustard seed
0.67 Tbsp cumin seed
4 bay leaves
2.67 tsp coarse sea salt

Shrimp Seasoning
0.33 tsp smoked paprika
1 tsp garlic powder
0.33 tsp mustard dry ground or substitute mustard seed
0.67 tsp sea salt
0.33 tsp pepper

STEPS TO COOK

1. Place the quartered onions in the inner pot. Cut the ends off of 3 ears of corn and leave the husks on. Place corn in the inner pot. Quarter the potatoes and place in the inner pot. Add in the whole spice seasoning blend. Add 2 cups of chicken stock.
2. Add in one bulb of garlic, peeled and smashed. Cut the Andouille sausage in 1/2 lengthwise on the diagonal and add to inner pot. Add in the Thyme and lemon cut in half
3. Pour about 1/2 cup of water over frozen shrimp and toss with shrimp seasoning. Add to inner pot. Cut the zucchini in half and place in pot.
4. Put the pressure lid on and turn the valve to seal. Set the pressure on high for 2 minutes. When the time is up removing the lid.
5. Melt the Cajun butter and pour over shrimp boil. Serve and Enjoy!
6. Cajun Butter
7. Blend room temp butter with seasonings.

Cajun Butter

0.67 cup salted butter 1 stick
1.33 tsp cumin ground
1.33 tsp brown sugar
1 tsp garlic powder
1 tsp onion powder
0.33 tsp smoked paprika
0.17 tsp chipotle ground

82. Herbed Salmon Recipe

TIME TO PREPARE
2

COOK TIME
5

SERVING
2

PREPARED BY NINJA FOODI

INGREDIENTS

8 oz. Sizzle Fish Salmon Filets, I used two, 4-oz Sizzle Fish Sockeye Salmon filets
1 tsp Herbs de Provence
1/4 tsp Natural Sea Salt
1/4 tsp Black Pepper
1/4 tsp Smoked Paprika
2 tbsp Olive Oil
1 tbsp Medlee Seasoned Butter, I used Medlee Lemon & Herb. You could swap this for regular butter and a squeeze of lemon juice.

STEPS TO COOK

1. Dry your filets with a paper towel and run the surface gently to ensure that there are no bones
2. Drizzle the olive oil on the fish and rub it in on both sides of the fix
3. Mix the seasonings & sprinkle them on both sides of the fish
4. Turn your air fryer on 390 degrees and cook for 5-8 minutes. I recommend starting with 5 minutes, checking the fish, and increasing the time by 1 additional minutes until it flakes easily with a fork.
5. Melt the seasoned butter for 30 seconds in the microwave and pour it over the fish before eating.

83. Fish and Grits

TIME TO PREPARE
10

COOK TIME
28

SERVING
2

PREPARED BY
Ninja foodi

INGREDIENTS

3 cups chicken broth
1 cup heavy cream
1 cup stone ground grits
2 Tbsp butter
1 tsp salt
2 pieces' tilapia fish
2 tsp blackened or Cajun seasoning
vegetable oil in a spray bottle

STEPS TO COOK

1. Place chicken broth, heavy cream, grits, salt and butter in Ninja Foodi pressure cooker insert. Stir. Cover with pressure cooker cover. Make sure valve is set to "Seal."
2. Cook on High Pressure for 8 minutes. Once 8 minutes is up, allow the Ninja Foodi to natural release for 10 minutes. Press cancel and release the remaining pressure by turning the valve to "Vent."
3. Meanwhile, season fish with blackened or Cajun seasoning by first spraying the fish, then rubbing the seasoning into both sides of the fish.
4. Once all pressure is released, open Foodi and stir grits. Place a piece of heavy-duty foil on top of the grits to cover. Lay the seasoned fish on top of the foil. Spray again with oil.
5. Close the Air Crisp lid on the ninja Foodi. Cook at 400 degrees Fahrenheit for 10 minutes or until fish can be easily flaked with a fork.
6. Serve fish over grits and Enjoy.

84. Air Fryer Tilapia

TIME TO PREPARE
15

COOK TIME
5

SERVING
5

PREPARED BY NINJA FOODI

INGREDIENTS

4 fish fillets tilapia, previously frozen and defrosted
1 c Italian bread crumbs
1 1/2 tbsp Old Bay or seafood magic seasoning
1 egg whisked
olive oil spray

STEPS TO COOK

1. Preheat air fryer to 400 degrees. Dip fish fillet in egg, then press both sides into bread crumb mixture that has been combined with seafood seasoning on a plate.
2. Place inside air fryer basket. Do the same for your 2nd fillet. Do not overlap pieces.
3. Close lid and cook at 400 degrees for 4-6 minutes depending on the thickness of your tilapia and how well done you like it. 4 minutes was plenty for ours.

85. Crumbed Fish

TIME TO PREPARE
10

COOK TIME
12

SERVING
4

PREPARED BY
Ninja foodi

INGREDIENTS

1 cup dry bread crumbs1/4 cup vegetable oil
4 flounder fillets
1 egg, beaten
1 lemon, sliced

STEPS TO COOK

1. Preheat an air fryer to 350 degrees F (180 degrees C).
2. Mix bread crumbs and oil together in a bowl. Stir until mixture becomes loose and crumbly.
3. Dip fish fillets into the egg; shake off any excess. Dip fillets into the bread crumb mixture; coat evenly and fully.
4. Lay coated fillets gently in the preheated air fryer. Cook the fish for about 12 minutes. Garnish with lemon slices.

86. Beer Battered Fish

TIME TO PREPARE 10	**COOK TIME** 12	**SERVING** 4	**PREPARED BY NINJA FOODI**

INGREDIENTS

- 1 CUP all-purpose flour
- 2 TABLESPOONS cornstarch
- ½ TEASPOON baking soda
- 6 OUNCES beer
- 1 egg beaten
- ¾ CUP all-purpose flour
- ½ TEASPOON paprika
- 1 TEASPOON salt
- ¼ TEASPOON freshly ground black pepper
- PINCH cayenne pepper
- 1½ POUNDS cod cut into 4 or 5 pieces
- vegetable oil

STEPS TO COOK

1. Combine the 1 cup of flour, cornstarch and baking soda in a large bowl. Put the beer and egg and stir until smooth. Cover the bowl of batter with plastic wrap and refrigerate for at least 20 minutes.
2. Combine the 3/4 cup of flour, paprika, salt, black pepper and cayenne pepper in a shallow dredging pan.
3. Pat the cod fish fillets dry with a paper towel. Dip the fish into the batter, coating all sides. Let the excess batter drip off and then coat each fillet with the seasoned flour. Sprinkle any leftover flour on the fish fillets and pat gently to adhere the flour to the batter.
4. Pre-heat the air fryer to 390°F.
5. Generously spritz both sides of the coated fish filets with vegetable oil and place them in the air fryer basket. Air-fry for 12 minutes at 390ºF. Spritz with more oil during the cooking process if there are any dry spots on the coating.
6. Serve immediately with lemon wedges, malt vinegar and tartar sauce. It's perfect with some air-fried French fries and coleslaw too!

87. Lobster Tails

TIME TO PREPARE
5

COOK TIME
4

SERVING
4

PREPARED BY
Ninja foodi

INGREDIENTS

2 lobster tails (mine were about 1/2 lb./tail)
½ teaspoon salt
½ teaspoon pepper
1 cup water
1 tablespoon butter
pinch of garlic powder
2 tablespoons butter, melted
1 teaspoon paprika
Melted butter, for dipping (optional)

STEPS TO COOK

1. With a sharp, clean kitchen shears, cut the shell of the lobster tail right down the middle.
2. With both hands, pry the shell apart, loosening the meat of the lobster from the bottom, sides and top of the shell (keeping the end of the tail intact).
3. Once the meat is loosened, carefully pull the meat through the top of the shell and place it on top of the opened shell.
4. Season lobster meat with salt and pepper.
5. Add water and one tablespoon of butter to cooking pot.
6. Place Foodi rack in lower position in the pot and position lobster tails on rack.
7. Put pressure cooking lid on Foodi and make sure pressure release valve is in the SEAL position.
8. Select HIGH PRESSURE for 2 minutes. QUICK RELEASE.
9. Combine garlic powder and melted butter.
10. Brush tails with garlic butter mixture.
11. Sprinkle tails with paprika.
12. AIR CRISP at 375º Fahrenheit for two minutes, brushing tails again with garlic butter halfway through cook time.
13. Remove tails from Foodi and enjoy with melted butter.

88. Mahi Mahi with Peach & Arugula Salad

TIME TO PREPARE	COOK TIME	SERVING	PREPARED BY
10	15	1	NINJA FOODI

INGREDIENTS

- 2 Mahi Mahi filets (about 6 oz. each)
- 2 slices Dave's Killer Bread (21 Grains) or whole wheat bread of your choice
- 1/2 cup parmesan cheese, freshly grated
- 1 egg, large
- 1/2 tbsp milk
- 1/4 cup whole wheat flour
- 1 tbsp white balsamic vinegar
- 1 tbsp extra virgin olive oil
- 1/4 tsp Dijon mustard
- 3 cups arugula, lightly packed
- 2 peaches, pitted and sliced
- 1/4 cup red onion, thinly sliced

STEPS TO COOK

1. Toast bread in toaster oven until lightly browned. Break or cut into small cubes, place in a food processor and pulse until finely ground.
2. Add parmesan cheese to bread crumbs and stir until well combined. Set aside.
3. Whisk the eggs and milk together in a bowl and set aside.
4. Set up your "breading" station - one container or area (I put my dry ingredients on a strip of plastic wrap to cut down on dirty dishes) for the flour, one for the egg wash and one for the bread crumb and parmesan mixture.
5. Lightly season Mahi Mahi with salt and pepper. Coat in the flour, shaking off the excess before placing in the egg wash. After coating in the egg wash, place the filet in the breading and turn to coat. Repeat with remaining filet.
6. Power on the Ninja Foodi. Insert the "Cook & Crisp" basket and set the Ninja to the Air Crisp function at a temp of 390. Close crisping lid and allow the Foodi to preheat for 3 minutes prior to adding the Mahi Mahi.
7. While the Foodi heats up, whisk together the white balsamic, olive oil and Dijon mustard. Place peaches in a medium sized bowl and pour vinegar mixture over top. Toss to combine, and set aside.
8. Carefully add Mahi Mahi to the "Cook & Crisp" basket. Allow to cook at 390 for 10 minutes, or until done.
9. Add arugula and red onion to peaches and toss until well combined. Serve immediately.

89. Fish Recipe Pecan Crusted Halibut

TIME TO PREPARE
15

COOK TIME
10

SERVING
4

PREPARED BY
Ninja foodi

INGREDIENTS

4 4-oz Halibut filets skin removed
1/2 cup pecan pieces
1/2 cup panko breadcrumbs
2 tablespoons lemon pepper divided
2 egg whites
1/2 cup cornstarch
1/2 cup white wine
Lemon wedges

STEPS TO COOK

1. Prepare the dredge by whisking together the cornstarch with egg whites
2. Add white wine a tablespoon at a time to the dredge until it's about the consistency of pancake batter
3. Add lemon pepper to the dredge and stir
4. Using a food processor, break down the pecan pieces until they are the consistency of breadcrumbs
5. Combine the pecan crumbs and panko on a bowl and stir to combine
6. Season each of the halibut filets with salt and lemon pepper
7. Dredge the halibut into the egg mixture and then into the pecan breadcrumbs making sure the fish is well crusted
8. Repeat with remaining fish
9. Preheat your air fryer to 375F
10. Cook the pecan-crusted halibut in the air fryer for about 8 minutes or until it has reached an internal temperature of 140F
11. Serve with a lemon wedge

90. Air Fryer Catfish

TIME TO PREPARE
7

COOK TIME
20

SERVING
4

PREPARED BY
NINJA FOODI

INGREDIENTS

4 Catfish Fillets or Catfish Nuggets
1/2 Cup Gluten Free Fish Fry
Olive Oil Cooking Spray

STEPS TO COOK

1. Coat each catfish fillet or nugget with an even coat of fish fry.
2. Place in the air fryer and spray the olive oil spray on one side of the catfish.
3. Cook at 390* for 10 minutes.
4. Carefully flip the catfish, coat with spray, and cook for an additional 10 minutes.
5. Serve.

91. Crispy Golden Air Fryer Fish

TIME TO PREPARE	**COOK TIME**	**SERVING**	**PREPARED BY**
2	14	2	NINJA FOODI

INGREDIENTS

Air Fryer Fish Fillets
2 tbsp cornmeal polenta
2 tsp Cajun seasoning
½ tsp paprika
½ tsp garlic powder
sea salt flakes to taste
2 catfish fillets
low calorie spray

STEPS TO COOK

1. Preheat air fryer to 400F (200C).
2. Mix the first 5 ingredients together and then add to a Ziploc bag.
3. Rinse the catfish, pat dry and add fillets to the Ziploc bag.
4. Seal the bag and then shake until the fillets are fully coated.
5. Place the coated fillets in the air fryer basket. (if you have a small fryer you will need to cook them one at a time).
6. Spray the fillets with low calorie spray, close the air fryer and cook for 10 Mins.
7. Turn the air fried fish fillets over and cook for an additional 3-4 Mins, or until done.

Chapter Sex Desserts

92. Chocolate Fondue

TIME TO PREPARE
5

COOK TIME
30

SERVING
7

PREPARED BY NINJA FOODI

INGREDIENTS

1 bag (12 ounces) semi-sweet chocolate chips
1 cup heavy cream

STEPS TO COOK

1. Place chocolate chips and heavy cream in the blender pitcher.
2. Select SAUCE/DIP.
3. Serve fondue warm with pretzels, marshmallows, strawberries, or other fruit, as desired.

93. Broiled Bananas

TIME TO PREPARE
5

COOK TIME
8

SERVING
4

PREPARED BY
NINJA FOODI

INGREDIENTS

2 tablespoons dark brown sugar

1 teaspoon ground cinnamon

2 firm medium-sized bananas, cut in half lengthwise

Toppings

Walnuts, chopped

Whipped cream

Sprinkles

Chocolate syrup

STEPS TO COOK

1. In a small bowl, mix brown sugar and cinnamon. Rub the mixture onto the bananas, then place the bananas on the Ninja pan.
2. Select AIR BROIL-LO and set time to 6 minutes. Press START/PAUSE to begin.
3. After 6 minutes, check bananas for doneness. Tops of bananas should be caramelized. If necessary, return pan to oven for 2 more minutes.
4. When cooking is complete, remove pan from oven and allow to cool for 5 minutes. Add desired toppings and serve immediately.

94. Grilled Strawberry Shortcake Skewers

TIME TO PREPARE	COOK TIME	SERVING	PREPARED BY
20	46	5	NINJA FOODI

INGREDIENTS

- 1 box classic white cake mix
- 1 cup premade vanilla pudding (optional)
- Cooking spray
- 2 cups strawberries, cut in half, stems removed
- 1/4 cup granulated sugar
- 2 tablespoons honey
- 5 skewers
- Whipped cream, for serving
- Vanilla ice cream, for serving

STEPS TO COOK

1. Mix cake batter according to the instructions on the box (if desired, substitute the 1 cup of water with 1 cup premade vanilla pudding for a cake that is denser and better able to stand up to high-temperature grilling).
2. Remove grill grate from unit and close hood. Select BAKE, set temperature to 325°F, and set time to 40 minutes. Select START/STOP to begin preheating.
3. While the unit is preheating, liberally coat the Ninja® multi-purpose pan* (or an 8-inch baking pan) with cooking spray. Pour batter into the pan.
4. When the unit has beeps to signify it has preheated, place the pan in the pot. Close hood and cook for 40 minutes.
5. Meanwhile, place the strawberries in a mixing bowl and toss them with sugar until well coated. Let them sit for 5 to 10 minutes, then add honey and mix well to coat. Set strawberries aside.
6. When cooking is complete, allow the cake to cool for 15 to 20 minutes, then remove it from the pan and use a serrated knife to cut it into 2" x 2" cubes. Assemble the skewers alternating between cake cubes and strawberries. Reserve the liquid from the strawberries.
7. Insert grill grate in unit and close hood. Select GRILL, set temperature to HIGH, and set time to 6 minutes. Select START/STOP to begin preheating.
8. While the unit is preheating, spray each skewer with cooking spray.
9. When the unit has beeps to signify it has preheated, place skewers on the grill grate. Close hood and cook for 3 minutes.
10. After 3 minutes, flip skewers over, close hood, and cook for 3 more minutes.
11. When cooking is complete, transfer skewers to a serving plate. Spoon strawberry liquid over the top and serve with whipped cream and/or vanilla ice cream.

94. Zeppole

 **TIME TO PREPARE** 30

 COOK TIME 24

 SERVING 12

 PREPARED BY NINJA FOODI

INGREDIENTS

- 1/4 cup water
- 1 teaspoon active dry yeast
- 2 tablespoons sugar
- 2 cups all-purpose flour
- 1/2 cup whole-milk ricotta cheese
- 1 large egg
- Zest of 1 orange
- 1 teaspoon vanilla extract
- 3/4 teaspoon kosher salt
- 1/4 teaspoon freshly grated nutmeg
- 1 1/2 sticks (3/4 cup) unsalted butter, softened, divided
- Confectioners' sugar, for dusting

STEPS TO COOK

1. Warm water to 110° F, then combine with yeast and 1 teaspoon sugar in the bowl of a stand mixer and let sit until mixture becomes foamy, about 5 minutes.
2. Add flour, ricotta, egg, orange zest, vanilla, salt, nutmeg, and remaining 2 tablespoons sugar, and attach bowl to stand mixer fitted with dough hook attachment. Mix on low speed until the dough forms.
3. Gradually add 1/2 cup butter, one tablespoon at a time, occasionally stopping mixer to scrape down sides of bowl. Increase speed to medium and beat until dough is cohesive, smooth, and glossy, about 4 minutes. If necessary, scrape dough from hook and sides of bowl. Remove bowl from mixer, cover with plastic wrap and let rise at room temperate for 2 hours.
4. Transfer dough to a lightly floured surface and shape into a smooth ball. 12 equal portions and roll into tight balls. Place on a baking sheet and let sit covered at room temperature for 30 minutes.
5. After 30 minutes, close crisping lid. Preheat the unit by selecting AIR CRISP, setting the temperature to 360°F, and setting the time to 3 minutes. Select START/STOP to begin.
6. Melt remaining 1/4 cup butter. Brush half the dough balls with melted butter and place them in the Cook & Crisp™ Basket. Reserve unused butter.
7. Once unit has preheated, place basket in pot. Close lid. Select AIR CRISP, set temperature to 350°F, and set time to 10 minutes. Select START/STOP to begin.
8. Cooking is complete when Zeppole are deep golden brown. Remove them from basket, brush again with melted butter, and sprinkle with confectioners' sugar.
9. Repeat steps 6 through 8 with remaining dough balls. Serve warm.

95. Coconut Pineapple Sorbet

TIME TO PREPARE
10

FREEZE
3H

SERVING
4

PREPARED BY
Ninja foodi

INGREDIENTS

140 g frozen pineapple chunks
1 small frozen ripe banana
1 tablespoon fresh lime juice
125 ml light coconut milk
1 tablespoon agave nectar
1 teaspoon grated fresh ginger

STEPS TO COOK

1. Place all ingredients into the 2.1 L Total Crushing Pitcher in the order listed.
2. Select ICE CREAM.
3. Remove mixture from pitcher and place in the freezer for at least 15 minutes before serving. For a consistency of hard ice cream, put it in the freezer for 2-3 hours or until hardened.

96. Spicy Mango Sorbet

TIME TO PREPARE 5	**COOK TIME** 0	**SERVING** 7	**PREPARED BY** NINJA FOODI

INGREDIENTS

- 4 cups frozen mango chunks
- 1 1/2 cups coconut milk
- 1/4 teaspoon cayenne pepper
- 2 tablespoons agave nectar

STEPS TO COOK

1. Place all ingredients in 88-ounce Blender Pitcher.
2. Select BOOST YES Auto-iQ TOTAL CRUSH.

97. Mocha

TIME TO PREPARE
5

COOK TIME
0

SERVING
2

PREPARED BY NINJA FOODI

INGREDIENTS

1/2 cup plus 1 tablespoon double-strength brewed coffee, chilled
2 cups ice
1/4 cup 1% milk
1/4 cup chocolate syrup, plus more for garnish
Whipped cream, for garnish

STEPS TO COOK

1. Place all ingredients, except whipped cream, into the 24-ounce Tritan Nutri Ninja Cup in the order listed.
2. Select Auto-iQ BOOST YES SMOOTHIE.
3. Remove blades from cup after blending.
4. Divide between 2 glasses, top with whipped cream, and drizzle with chocolate syrup.

98. Lemon Strawberry Sorbet

| **TIME TO PREPARE** 5 | **COOK TIME** 0 | **SERVING** 4 | **PREPARED BY** NINJA FOODI |

INGREDIENTS

- 3 cups frozen strawberries
- 1 1/2 cups lemonade

STEPS TO COOK

1. Place all ingredients into the 40-ounce Processor Bowl in the order listed.
2. BLEND until smooth.

99. Cranberry Salsa over Cream Cheese

TIME TO PREPARE	COOK TIME	SERVING	PREPARED BY
5	0	2	NINJA FOODI

INGREDIENTS

- 14 oz. can whole cranberry sauce
- 1 tablespoon fresh cilantro
- 1 green onion, cut in half
- 1 jalapeno pepper, seeded and cut in half
- 1/3 cup lime juice
- Pinch of salt
- 8 oz. block of reduced fat cream cheese

STEPS TO COOK

1. Place ingredients, except cream cheese, into the 40 oz. blender and pulse 6-8 times.
2. Place the cream cheese on a serving dish, and then pour the cranberry salsa over top. Serve with tortilla chips or crackers and enjoy.

100. Easy Crème Brulee

TIME TO PREPARE
0

COOK TIME
0

SERVING
0

PREPARED BY
Ninja foodi

INGREDIENTS

1 3/4 cups heavy cream
1/3 cup plus 4 teaspoons sugar
3 egg yolks
1 teaspoon vanilla extract
2 cups water

STEPS TO COOK

1. Pour heavy cream into microwavable bowl. Microwave on HIGH 3 minutes. Whisk in 1/3 cup sugar until sugar is dissolved. Slowly whisk 1/3 cup warm cream into egg yolks in another bowl. Whisk yolk mixture back into remaining cream mixture. Stir in vanilla extract. Pour cream mixture into 4 (6-ounce) ramekins.

2. Pour water into pot. Place roasting rack into pot and place ramekins on rack. Set OVEN to 325°F for 1 hour. Cover with lid and cook until just set. Remove ramekins from pot and let cool. Cover ramekins and refrigerate 2 hours.

3. Remove ramekins from refrigerator and let stand 20 minutes. Sprinkle remaining sugar over custards in ramekins. Use small cooking torch to caramelize the sugar, forming a candy shell.

www.ingramcontent.com/pod-product-compliance
Lightning Source LLC
Chambersburg PA
CBHW081402070526
44583CB00020B/2642